Mom
Matters

JANE JARRELL

HARVEST HOUSE PUBLISHERS
Eugene, Oregon 97402

Cover by Left Coast Design, Portland, Oregon

Published in Association with the literary agency of Alive Communications, Inc., 7680 Goddard Street, Suite 200, Colorado Springs, CO 80920.

Some material was taken from *Holiday Hugs* (Harvest House Publishers, 2000); *Love You Can Touch* (Harvest House Publishers, 1999); and *26 Ways to Say "I Love You"* (Harvest House Publishers, 2000) by Jane Jarrell.

MOM MATTERS
Copyright © 2001 by Jane Jarrell
Published by Harvest House Publishers
Eugene, Oregon 97402

Library of Congress Cataloging-in-Publication Data

Jarrell, Jane Cabaniss
    Mom matters / Jane Jarrell.
        p. cm.
    ISBN 0-7369-0497-2
    1. Family.   2. Family recreation.   3. Family—Religious life.   4 Mothers.   I. Title.
HQ515.J37 2001
306.85—dc21   00-061405

Printed in the United States of America

        01   02   03   04   05   06   07   / RDP-CF /   10   9   8   7   6   5   4   3   2   1

*For my mother, Sarah Hull Cabaniss,
who has and will always matter,
from generation to generation.*

Acknowledgments

My heartfelt thanks go to…

Mark and Sarah—you two matter most! Your love, support, and encouragement make up my light at the end of the tunnel.

Kim Moore—we did it, thanks to you!

Leah Dawn Eiden—for not being afraid to use that purple pen. Your notes of encouragement and the silver cross remind me God is still in control in the midst of computer crashes, family illnesses, and other manuscripts needing attention. Your help cannot be measured.

Kelly McBrayer, Mary Sheppard, Deborah Saathoff, Allegra Jarrell, Susie Jarrell, and Charlie, Damita and Chelsey Cabaniss—for inviting Sarah over for playdates, swimming afternoons, trips to Chuck E. Cheese, peanut butter and jelly sandwich lunches, and much more. You made it possible for me to work knowing Sarah was safe, loved, and having fun.

Dr. Rochelle Reed Brunson—for the numerous phone calls, prayers, encouragement, and friendship.

My parents—your love, support, consistent encouragement, and so much more always mean so much.

Edwina and R.J., Elizabeth and Craig Berry, and Andrew and Amy Burns—our once-a-month prayer group. Thank you for your prayers, love, e-mails, and cards.

The AttaGirls—for your contribution to this book. You are a lovely group of mothers, authors, speakers, and encouragers sent straight from God.

Carolyn McCready and Barb Sherrill—for coming to Dallas and offering me encouragement and the idea. May God bless you.

Chip MacGregor—agent, writer, and editor. Thank you for believing in me.

Contents

Life Matters

Husbands Matter

Ways to Help Him Be the Spiritual Leader of Your Home ❧ Ways to Capture Husband-and-Wife Teamwork ❧ Great Ideas for Thrill'n Grill'n ❧ Great Birthday Surprises ❧ Super Dates ❧ Ways to Keep Love Alive ❧ Fight Diffusers ❧ Little "Happys" That Say "I Love You" ❧ Down-Home Tips for Worn-Out Marriages ❧ Ways to Offer Unexpected Encouragement ❧ Ways to Offer Significant Support to Your Husband ❧ Great Make-Ahead Meals He Will Love

Children Matter

Birthday Party Ideas, Percolating with Pizzazz ❧ Ways to Bring Your Child's Favorite Books to Life ❧ Ways to Corral Clutter ❧ Ways to Create a Space for Imaginations to Soar ❧ Quick and Cute Teacher Gifts ❧ Car Games for Adventurous Travelers ❧ Activities for Your Kids While You Prepare Dinner ❧ Ways to Make Bible Verse Memory Fun and Exciting ❧ Ways to Teach Your Child the Art of Sharing ❧

Reach Out to Your Neighbors ❧ Ways to Simplify Sharing ❧ Ways to Shop and Share ❧ Easy Friendship Baskets ❧ Signature Wraps That Say "I Love You" ❧ Hospitality Helpers ❧ Easy, Elegant, and Extravagant Easter ideas ❧ Family Traditions That Last a Lifetime ❧ Steps to an Organized Household ❧ Strategies for Having More Family Time ❧ Ideas for Thanksgiving Treats ❧ Homemade and Heartfelt Christmas Traditions ❧ Ways to Be a Good Mom and a Good Friend Too

Mom Matters
189

Ways to Make God First in Your Life ❧ Ways to Grow in God's Grace ❧ Ways to Find Joy ❧ Words of Encouragement to Help You Seize the Day ❧ Ways to Realness ❧ Simple Principles to Building Your Home with Encouragement and Love ❧ Ways to Establish Personal Peace ❧ Steps to Greater Health ❧ Ways to Transition to a "Stay-at-Home" Mom ❧ Things to Consider When You Have a "Working from Home" Office ❧ Ways to Streamline and Style-up Your Wardrobe ❧ "Little Luxuries" to Celebrate You ❧ Ways to Take a Daily Mini Vacation ❧ Ways to Achieve the Spirit of Femininity ❧ Ways to Stay in Shape ❧ Makeup Secrets to Keep You Cute ❧ Ways to Build Speaking Confidence ❧ Things Moms Need Most

What Matters Most?
219

Recommended Resources
221

Life Matters

My, how time flies when you are getting older! As I reflect on bits and pieces of my life, I repeatedly focus fondly on the homes I have lived in, from those of my childhood to the one that shelters me now. The dictionary defines "home" as one's residence. To me, the word "home" means so much more. In school, students are grouped by homeroom. In business, employees obtain information from the home office. While cooking, we prefer home-grown fruits and vegetables. In baseball, you are safe when you reach home plate. You not only scored, but worked hard, ran fast, and need refreshment. Home should be a place for receiving what you need—relaxation, rejuvenation, and restoration.

As wives and mothers, we set the tone for our home. We are in the business of growing hearts while preventing damage from weeds the world blows into our garden. The responsibility can be overwhelming at times, but we are

God's chosen people for this extraordinary task. I desperately want my home to be a safe haven, a retreat, a breathing space to regroup, and a loving place to repair the damage the world throws our way.

Mom Matters is divided into five sections: Husbands Matter, Children Matter, Home Matters, Family and Friends Matter, and Mom Matters. Each section is filled with ideas on turning your home into the refuge your family needs.

My family, just like your family, has our ups and downs, our good times and bad, our trials and errors. As a family, we certainly do not do it all right, but we strive for God's best; we mess up, we jump up, we dust ourselves off, and we try again. It is my prayer that some of these ideas will add spice, create joy, and make a difference in your home as they have in ours.

Home and church have occupied an intertwined place in my heart. My parents worked in church for the first ten years of my life, so church was merely an extension of our home. My dad was an active Minister of Music and Education. Mom was a grade school teacher, choir member, and Sunday school teacher. She basically helped with anything and everything needed at church. If you have never been in church work, it is difficult to realize the 24-hour-a-day work experience, one in which the entire family plays a role. Ministering by choice becomes your lifestyle, your home a respite where many come to rejuvenate, relax, and refresh. This lifestyle made church and home so united that one would flow into the other.

I invited Christ into my heart when I was eight. The magnitude of choosing my eternal life's direction was discussed and accepted at home—a place where I felt loved and secure.

> In My Father's house are many dwelling places; if it were not so, I would have told you; for I go to prepare a place for you. And if I go and prepare a place for you, I will come again, and receive you to Myself; that where I am, there you may be also (John 14:2,3).

When my parents chose to leave full-time church work, Dad entered graduate school to obtain a doctorate. This moved our ministry lifestyle from the church into a marriage and family therapy career and soon led our family to Southern Illinois.

My younger brother, Charles, and I grew up on a 40-acre farm just outside of Marion, Illinois. It was a wonderful place. Mini-bikes, an ice-skating pond, rolling hills, and a huge swimming pool made our home a popular gathering place for family, friends, and church members. My favorite spot was the screened-in back porch. It was a plant haven with rocking chairs and a big swing. I loved to lie on that swing and just listen to the water ripple and the birds sing. Many special memories were made on that farm. But the best was the inviting warmth that made life serene and filled with bliss.

During my early teens and prior to leaving home for college, my brother and I had many jobs helping around the farm. A two-lane winding highway brought you from our small town to our house, located down a long drive-way bordered by an equally long white fence. This rolling white fence some how needed a good painting every summer. As Tom Sawyer knew, friend recruitment was a must. Our catchy slogan was "What a great way to get a tan!" The job was hot, messy, and sweaty, but always fun with family, friends, a very loud jam box, and an occa-sional jump in the pool. Thinking back, I recall the days our friends did not buy the "great way to get a tan" pitch were days that my brother and I really talked. We would share our hearts, sing at the top of our voices, and then talk some more. Those fence-painting times, as well as many others, paved the road for a lifelong friendship with my brother.

Leaving home for college brought inner strife. Part of me was ready to take on the world; the other part of me was afraid to leave home. Numerous family prayer times, college entrance forms, and recommendation letters became a part of our life. After various campus visits, I chose Baylor University in Waco, Texas, 800 miles from home.

God's calling on my life was first heard at college. Though Baylor has a lovely, tree-lined campus and offers a superb education, the little dorm rooms needed *imme-diate* interior design assistance. I think it was the cinder blocks, linoleum floors, and down-the-hall bathroom stalls that just did not meet my taste in up-to-date decor.

So I tried to fix my room up with the help of my deco-rator man of many talents, Dad. Posters, stereo, matching bedspreads, even padded and fabric-covered walls made a vast improvement, but it never was home.

Yet far from home blessings come in unexpected ways! Mine were several doors down the ugly hallway, inside equally unattractive dormitory rooms. There were girls, as unsure of their new surroundings as I, launching into the world of adulthood. Many of the ladies on the second floor of Collins dormitory are to this day some of my best friends. Once comfortable with our new world, we let our hair down and became a fun-loving group that had quite the reputation for loud laughter, long *Soul Train* dance sessions, and tricks that terrorized our dorm mother.

Though I began my studies in radio, television, and film, I rotated to fashion merchandising, and then landed in the Home Economics department. I graduated from Baylor with a bachelor of science degree in Home Economics Education. My first job was a freelance fashion show coordinator for a city-wide fashion show. I worked with the *Waco Tribune-Herald* selling advertising space to local retailers. The size of the ad determined how many outfits the store could have in the show. Once this was decided, I went to every store and selected the best clothes. After the clothes were chosen, I hired the models—college roommates, sorority sisters, and old boyfriends. Would you believe that it is truly hard work convincing people to walk down a runway all dressed up? Even after choosing models and clothing, we were only halfway there. The show lineup was developed, a commentator was chosen, the show was rehearsed innumerable times, and, finally, showtime! I directed the fashion show with 50-plus models for an audience of over 1,000. I was literally flying by the seat of my fashionable pants. Now, it was time for a real job.

Working with the newspaper provided the opportunity to meet the cooking show team from *Southern Living* magazine. After learning that one of the ladies was leaving the show group, I applied for the job. An interview in Dallas led to disappointment; I was not selected. I went immediately to Neiman Marcus and applied for a position in their epicure department—hopefully to be selected for the buyers' training program within a few months. I became the assistant manager for epicure in the downtown Neiman Marcus store. (I was very excited! On my fourteenth birthday, two of my presents were books written by Stanley Marcus: *Minding the Store* and *Quest for the Best.*)

As 21-year-old college graduates ready to take on the world, two of my college friends and I rented a "dorm unattractive" apartment in Dallas. Our lives consisted of riding the city bus downtown to work, shopping at least once a week at our favorite discount fashion store, and jogging each night in the most exclusive neighborhood in Dallas. We always wondered what those folks in the big mansions did for a living.

One busy day at the BIG (Neiman Marcus) store, I received a phone call from the lady who had interviewed me at *Southern Living.* She wanted to interview me again! Having my fashion dreams a bit jaded from the reality of the "real" work world, I felt an opportunity to work at a magazine would be incredible. I interviewed locally, then flew to the headquarters in Birmingham, Alabama, for two more days of grueling interviews. I toured their facilities, tasted cakes in their famous kitchens, dined in some fabulous restaurants, and (hallelujah) was offered the position of program coordinator for cooking shows. As I was going to be flying, traveling, renting cars, and running shows, all I needed now was a credit card!

What a blessing this job was. Though it was a hard time, it was a growing time. We did cooking shows all over the South to audiences averaging between 2,000–3,000. I would set up the events and emcee the shows. It was an overwhelming experience at 22, but it was an experience that continues to open doors for me to this day.

The magazine days heightened my interest in the areas of photography, selecting dish patterns, table accessories, colors, and food styling. Those beautiful pictures were brought together by somebody. Combining shopping, eating, and arranging pretty pictures sounded exciting to me. So, for many years I have been a food stylist, a.k.a. one who glues sesame seeds onto buns, thus making perfectly good food inedible but pretty. This adventure has included film shoots, magazine layouts, television commercials, and at least a million trips to various grocery stores. Incidentally, not a bit of this is glamorous. You smell like the food you have been working with, sometimes for days, and you stand on concrete floors for 12 to 16 hours making the same dish repeatedly. Yet even with all the hard work, I still find it interesting and do work periodically for the *Dallas Morning News* food section.

Careers are tremendous challenges, but relationships are the ultimate. Many times, life's road takes some interesting turns. I fell in what I call "runner up" love several times during college. I was dropped (means you wore a necklace with fraternity letters hanging from a gold chain), pinned (same letters just not on a necklace), and asked to go steady or whatever they call it now. But I have come to realize love, if chosen correctly, is God's greatest gift. My good friend Deborah said in an encouraging letter, "Love is like a hothouse flower: something that must be nurtured, protected, and cared about."

Little did I know that I would meet my forever partner on a blind date. My roommate, Monica, set me up with a tall, dark, and handsome guy with an appreciation for humor because she thought we had shared interests. We certainly did have things in common (more on this in the husband section)!

After I married Mark, the home became increasingly vital. Perhaps it is that nesting thing you hear about or love overflowing from a solid relationship that alters your interests and goals. Occupying our first residence, buying our first sofa, and looking at a shared future rebooted those home genes that were a bit latent because of career choices, poor past love decisions, low finances, and cinder block surroundings.

Early in our married life, I accepted food styling jobs whenever possible and returned to a full-time position with Neiman Marcus. This time I was the menu, promotions and advertising coordinator for 35 restaurants. Creating menus, plate presentations, and promotions to interest customers was a new field with familiar roots. This turned out to be my last full-time position prior to full-fledged motherhood.

Shortly after moving into our first house, our precious Sarah was born and our lives kicked into the amazing world of unknowns—moving faster than a sleepy speeding bullet and leaping tall diaper pails. For me, motherhood made every other experience in the world pale in comparison.

My prayers for wisdom increased. Holding a precious six-pound bundle of baby girl caused my mind to race. How would we nurture this child? What could we do to ensure her home was a happy one? How could we instill strong Christian values while making her home a haven?

Have you ever had these thoughts? If so, you are one whose heart is at home, who desires the best for your children, and who looks for ideas to follow God's direction for your life and the life of your family.

The plot thickens in the Husbands Matter section. You will see idea after idea, all transferable to your family, from which you can pick and choose or use as a springboard to create your own.

So, come on, let's share some thoughts sprinkled with pearls of wisdom from godly people who have already accomplished "the happy home" and are actually living to tell about it.

When the heart goes before, like a lamp, and illumines the pathway, many things are made clear that else lie hidden in the darkness.

Longfellow

Husbands Matter

- ❤ 5 Ways to Help Him Be the Spiritual Leader of your Home

- ❤ 10 Ways to Capture Husband-and-Wife Teamwork

- ❤ 2 Great Ideas for Thrill'n Grill'n

- ❤ 12 Great Birthday Surprises

- ❤ 10 Super Dates

- ❤ 15 Ways to Keep Love Alive

- ❤ 5 Fight Diffusers

- ❤ 10 Little "Happys" That Say "I Love You"

- ❤ 6 Down-Home Tips for Worn-Out Marriages

- ❤ 10 Ways to Offer Unexpected Encouragement

- ❤ 5 Ways to Offer Significant Support to Your Husband

- ❤ 5 Great Make-Ahead Meals He Will Love

Husbands Matter

I am my beloved's and my beloved is mine.
Song of Solomon 6:3

As I moved into my twenties, a move was in order from my first big-city apartment into a more civilized duplex. Little did I know that on a late summer evening, standing on the other side of my duplex front door would be Mark, the blind date I now call husband and friend.

Mark is the master date-planner. I had never been out before with a man who not only frequented trendy restaurants but actually knew how to pronounce the dishes. Mr. GQ kept abreast of current clothing styles and wore them, had impeccable manners, and treated me like a queen. Our time together as a hot dating item was always an exciting adventure into all the pleasures of big city life: live theater, art museums, concerts, dancing, and romancing.

Did I mention he has a unique and keen sense of humor? Listen to this story. When we began dating, I was working for *Southern Living* magazine. One evening he invited me to his apartment for dinner, a dinner he had created himself. It was lovely: beef Wellington en croute, garlic new potatoes, fresh field greens tossed in a balsamic vinaigrette, julienne strips of carrots, squash, and zucchini, and the grand finale, a four-inch-high cheesecake with fresh berries for dessert. The table was exquisite, and the dinner was, frankly, intimidating. Glancing into the kitchen, I noticed several piles of dirty dishes, the sign of one who had expended a heroic effort in dining preparation. I was totally impressed, so, true to my nature, the gushing began. I went on and on about his culinary abilities. As my compliments and accolades waned, this funny grin came over his face. Being in true dating mode and wanting to understand everything about him, I began to question this response. Finally, he burst out laughing, escorted me to the refrigerator, and showed me all of the gourmet take-out containers he had hidden plus the mock-up dirty pots and pans that shined with the look of a greasy mess. Basically, I got took.

To make matters worse, he found this sooo funny that he wrote a letter to my boss. As a *Southern Living* executive, she felt it her mission in life to educate her staff in the finer points of *haute cuisine* by lecturing from the head of a table in the South's most exclusive restaurants. Mark explained to her that he was concerned about my inability to discern take-out from food prepared in an actual home kitchen and stated he feared I might not realize the difference between ground bologna and foie gras. I would have been mortified if I had not been laughing so hard when my boss read the letter to me. And this was just one of the many hilarious letters Mark wrote to me, my parents, and my friends on special occasions. There was even one to Elvis Presley, supposedly written by myself, begging him to let me audition as a backup singer.

The holidays seemed to make Mark's creative writing skills glisten. Our first Christmas came after we had been dating about four months. I was flying home to spend the holidays with my family in Southern Illinois. Mark volunteered to take me to the airport and see me off—as always, trying to make life easier for me. He presented me with a series of numbered gifts with strict instructions to open them in sequential order. I was so excited that Christmas morning, wondering what he could have possibly bought me and confident that whatever he had chosen would be beautiful (probably expensive) and sure to impress my parents! I eagerly tore open the wrapping from package number one and found a Neiman Marcus box with a note taped to it. I ignored the note and opened the box, sure I would find a gorgeous designer blouse or sweater. Much to my surprise, there was a hideous green polyester dress inside that he had purchased at a Goodwill store. The note described the dress in glowing detail as if it came off the pages of *Vogue* magazine. This pattern continued as I found matching green pumps a sensible grandmother might wear, plastic fish earrings (he noted the Christian symbolism for me), and a purple suede belt that was about five sizes too large. The last present I opened was actually something elegant, although for the life of me, I cannot remember the "real" gift, only the funny ones. One might think the story ends there with a good laugh for my family and me. But, Mark was not the only one with a sense of humor. You should have seen the look on his face when I stepped off the plane in Dallas wearing each and every piece of the ensemble. He quickly recovered from the shock and told me, "I'm so glad you wore the outfit. My parents are with me and are dying to meet you." He had the last laugh. His parents were not at the airport, but I was temporarily stricken with a terrible image of his genteel mother making some vain attempt at a compliment like, "What a wonderful retro dress" or "It's not everyone who can wear pea green."

Great dates, silly practical jokes, and time together makes dating and courtship sparkle with anticipation and fun. Mark received the credit card bills, and I never knew how much those events set him back. But they were sound investments.

It was those wonderful dates, long talks, and shared interests that led us to a lifelong commitment. We were to marry at the Dallas Arboretum with dozens of pink roses gracing the gazebo, a peaceful lake in the background, our guests strolling through the grounds, and the scene set for the perfect wedding. Now, if I had just avoided that nasty hemorrhaging and unanticipated trip to the emergency room, we would have driven off into the sunset. In the real world, we had to postpone our wedding until I recovered. I was told the seated luncheon was delightful. My matron of honor occupied my chair, just as though she were the first runner-up in a pageant, while my dad sat on the other side of Mark, who stared at the surreal scene in a daze, trying to comprehend that the wedding had not happened.

We had a rough start, to put it mildly. Our honeymoon was postponed, and our lives stayed in limbo until we dusted ourselves off and began again. Thank God, it is in the tough times that love sweetens. Thank God, that is what we experienced. We married in Mark's parents' home three weeks later with a different cake, decor, minister, and even a new best man. Finally, our journey began as husband and wife.

Today, we try to incorporate many of the following thoughts and suggestions into our life—we are still growing, learning, and attempting to treat our love as something to treasure.

❤ 5 Ways to Help Him Be the Spiritual Leader of Your Home

1. Encourage him to be the spiritual leader at home. When he leads be ready to follow.

2. Pray for him daily. Pray for his safety, his productivity, his leadership of your family, and his spiritual success.

3. Encourage him to find an accountability partner, a guy he can be transparent with and one who shares his same beliefs in God, family, and church.

4. Help him make good use of his time. Time is critical to sustaining a spiritual walk. A husband's schedule is often hectic, long, and stressful.

5. Enthusiastically acknowledge his efforts.

💜 10 Ways to Capture Husband-and-Wife Teamwork

1. Develop a close relationship with God. Let that draw you close to one another.

2. Discuss and come to an agreement on goals for your relationship and for your family.

3. Build a bridge of intimacy by taking time to nurture your relationship with date nights, love notes, little gifts, messages of encouragement, and lots of listening.

4. Join a Bible study or prayer group together.

5. Make time for romantic moments that bond, such as a quiet walk, a candlelit dinner, a back rub after a day at the computer.

6. Find ways to maximize your communication. Read *The Five Love Languages* by Gary Chapman. Take time to understand how your spouse best receives love. If you understand this and are willing to make an effort, the dividends could be incredible.

7. Find a comfortable place for a "State of the Union" discussion. This is a time to review your goals as a married couple. Discuss your hopes and dreams for your family, take a fresh look at your lives together, thank God for His blessings, and pray for His future provisions.

8. Edwina Patterson explains in *Redeeming the Time With My Husband*: "Tender feelings die when daily consideration and kindnesses fall by the wayside. Appreciation is the heart of a beautiful marriage. It is one piece of the puzzle to accept him just as he is, it is another to appreciate." (Heart for the Home Ministries, www.heart-for-home.org.)

9. Make promises you can keep. The way you treat *any* relationship in the family will eventually affect *every* relationship in the family.

10. The marriage relationship is like "God's heavenly sandpaper"; it can soften the rough edges in your life. When you choose a teamwork mentality first as a couple, then as a family, you begin to go at life together.

💜 2 Great Ideas for Thrill'n Grill'n

Summer becomes official when the grill is fired up. The kitchen moves outdoors for a new twist to some old favorites. Dad is usually the grill master, so let's motivate Dad to get out there and experience the thrill of the grill. Grills are not kid friendly, but children can help with the preparation and a creation of the edibles. With a little help from Dad, a dining experience is born.

Fruits, cakes, potatoes, and pizza are all at home on the grill, so try these new ideas for sizzling scrumptuous meals during your Father's Day celebration or anytime of the year.

Recipes

Petite Pizza Magic

Things You'll Need:

wide spatula
cookie sheet
small bowls
cutting board
sharp knife or pizza cutter

Ingredients:

4 small store-bought prepared pizza doughs or dough
  made ahead
1 large jar spaghetti sauce
a parade of toppings:
  carrots
  pineapple
  ham
  bell pepper
  precooked chicken chunks
  broccoli
  olives
  pepperoni
  Parmesan cheese
  mozzarella cheese

Directions:

1. Place the prepared pizza dough on a cookie sheet; spread a layer of the spaghetti sauce over the entire surface of each round of dough.

2. Let everyone select his or her favorite toppings to be sprinkled on top of each pizza. You may want to suggest that the children fashion faces or shapes and give their personal creations special names.

3. Top with a sprinkling of cheese and place on a medium grill for 6 to 8 minutes. Serve with a side salad or fresh fruit.

❤ ❤ ❤

Recipes

Grilled Pound Cake

Things You'll Need:

cookie sheet
long grill spatula
pastry brush
small bowl

Ingredients:

1 store-bought pound cake
½ stick butter, melted
1 small jar marmalade, melted
½ cup milk chocolate chips

Directions:

1. Slice the pound cake into 1-inch slices; brush both sides of each slice with melted butter

2. Place each slice on a clean grill. Grill about 1 minute on each side.

3. Paint each slice with melted orange marmalade.

4. Place on a serving plate and sprinkle with chocolate chips.

♥   ♥   ♥

♥ 12 Great Birthday Surprises

1. Plan a road trip for your husband and a few of his best buddies. Adjust the specifics of the trip to his preferences.

2. Schedule an afternoon at a spa/health club that offers Swedish massage, a steam room, and a whirlpool.

3. Rent a bus or van to transport your friends to a sporting event. Have a tailgate birthday party.

4. Arrange for him to take lessons in something that interests him. Golf, art, cooking, drywalling, race-car driving...the possibilities are endless.

5. Buy an item autographed by his personal hero. Baseballs, letters, and pictures can be treasured mementos.

6. Make him King for the Day. He gets to choose everything from menus to TV programs to what time he wakes up.

7. Give him a blast-from-the-past party. Try to locate high school friends he may not have seen in years. Keep each one behind a closed door and have them give him clues until he guesses their identities.

8. Set up a poker party for him and his best friends. Provide snacks and a bowl of pennies with which to "gamble." Leave them alone to stay up late and test their luck.

9. Send a large balloon bouquet to his office.

10. Create a children's party for adults in his honor, serve his favorite childhood foods, and ask guests to bring children's gifts to be donated to charity.

11. Organize a scavenger hunt to find presents. Fill an envelope with clues to help him find his gifts.

12. Prepare his favorite meal and serve it on your wedding china. Make the meal extra special with candles, soft music, and a children's night out.

💜 10 Super Dates

1. Have Chinese take-out delivered to your favorite park. Arrive earlier than your food order with a blanket, portable music player, and candles.

2. Plan a one-night excursion to a quaint bed-and-breakfast. Make this a time of total relaxation and

conversation so you can catch up on each other's thoughts and feelings.

3. Do a fast-food drive-through progressive dinner. Begin at one of your favorites for an appetizer and end up at another for dessert. When full, drop by a miniature golf course for a fun golf game.

4. Make reservations for an afternoon together at a day spa.

5. Plan an outing to the ocean, lake, pond, or river. Depending on your water source, enjoy a fun activity. You might end up in a canoe, a fishing boat, or an evening dinner cruise.

6. Check out your community theater offerings. If you are in close proximity to a major city, see if they have a ticket outlet for a great play or musical at a reasonable rate.

7. Experiment with new cuisines. Try a Thai, Vietnamese, or Lebanese restaurant. If you are the adventurous type, check out a sushi bar.

8. Plan a movie evening at home without the kids. Arrange for the children to stay elsewhere. Rent a romantic video you would love and an action-packed video for him. Pop some corn and snuggle on the couch.

9. For a special treat, check into a hot-air balloon ride. They usually take off at sunrise or sunset so the

romance is built in. If the balloon company does not provide refreshments, take a basket of fruit and cheese.

10. Recreate your first date as closely as possible. Go to the same restaurant, rent the same movie, or go to the same theater. If this is impossible, pretend this is your first date. Have your husband leave and come pick you up. Talk to each other as though you first met. Decide if you are going to let him kiss you or not!

Draw me after you and let us run together!
Song of Solomon 1:4

15 Ways to Keep Love Alive

1. Plan an unexpected getaway just for the two of you and organize the child care without complaining.

2. Say "I love you" often.

3. Wear lingerie that he likes. Save the flannel pajamas for the nights one of you has to be out of town.

4. Find something that interests both of you and take time to enjoy it.

5. Go out together at least twice a month, even if it is just for ice cream or coffee.

6. Make sure his last impression of you each morning is a positive one. Even if you do not plan to leave the

house that day, dress, put on a little makeup, comb your hair, brush your teeth, and give him a big hug and a kiss before he walks out the door.

7. Greet your spouse at the door when he comes home from work. Smile and tell him he was missed.

8. Limit your phone time when your husband is home. Save those long chats with girlfriends for when he is at work.

9. Tuck a small gift in his briefcase or lunch box that reflects something he enjoys. Golf balls, CDs, a new tool, chocolate—whatever makes him happy.

10. Meet him for lunch at a favorite restaurant on a work day.

11. Arrange for him to spend time with his buddies. Tickets for a baseball game, a new fishing reel, or a reservation for the racquetball court work wonders.

12. Massage his neck or feet while you watch television together.

13. Prepare his favorite dessert for no special reason.

14. Call a lawn service and surprise him with a weekend minus yard work.

15. Be sensitive with his moods. When you have something important to discuss with him, timing is critical. If at all possible, do not bring it up as he walks in the

door from work. Try to wait until after he has had a chance to unwind and eat a bite.

There is no more lovely, friendly, and charming relationship, communion, or company than a good marriage.

Martin Luther

💜 5 Fight Diffusers

1. Laugh with each other, especially after the issue has been resolved.

2. Establish a fighting time, so both of you can cool off and approach the topic with a level head instead of a hot head.

3. Listen to his side of the story instead of planning your next rebuttal.

4. Establish "time-outs" for checkups on your relationship. Ask simple questions like: How are you doing? How are you feeling about us?

5. Seek professional Christian counseling if the same issues resurface time and time again.

Do not let the sun go down on your anger.

Ephesians 4:26

❤ 10 Little "Happys" That Say "I Love You"

1. Send an "I love you" card to his office or try an e-card for a pleasant surprise in the middle of a hectic day.

2. Read *The Language of Love* by Gary Smalley and John Trent, Ph.D. Learn how to communicate in word pictures so your point of view can be understood.

3. Place a small box of chocolates in his briefcase.

4. Fill his car with gas when he would least expect it and most need it.

5. Have an art time with the kids and ask them to create a picture for Daddy's office. Roll up the picture and tie it with a ribbon.

6. Place a single red rose in a pretty bud vase on his bedside table.

7. Purchase a subscription to his favorite magazine or business journal.

8. Bake his favorite dessert for him to take to his office.

9. Give him an evening of complete relaxation. Take the kids somewhere and give him the remote or schedule a massage, manicure, or golf game.

10. Send a petite book of love poetry to his office. When he looks at it, he will know how much he is loved.

My heart to you is given. Oh, do give yours to me:
We'll lock them up together, and throw away the key.

Frederick Saunders

💜 6 Down-Home Tips for Worn-Out Marriages

Becky Freeman, mother, author, and speaker, has written many books. One of her latest is *Chocolate Chili Pepper Love*. In it she offers tips for marriages that need a little polish in order to sparkle.

1. Know when to yelp for help. In her book *Marriage* 911, Becky compared the feelings of hurting couples to those of accident victims. Seek godly counsel. Sometimes professional counseling is warranted.

2. Sweep the junk off the porch. "Have you ever fantasized about starting over with someone who doesn't have your background of faults stored in their personal files? Who hasn't? Sweep the junk off the porch with a broom of forgiveness."

3. Focus your lens on the roses, not the junk. "Focus on the good things about your mate. Focus on the roses, and they'll loom so large and beautiful that quite often the junk disappears altogether from view."

4. Grow each other up. "There is a theory that we marry each other, in part, to help us finish childhood. Or as Joseph Barth said, 'Marriage is our last chance to grow up.' Inside, aren't we all still a little like toddlers? Especially when we are tired or our affection tanks are low."

5. Two parasites can't feed on each other. "I know this sounds gross, but it's a perfect picture of what happens when we expect another person to make us happy."

6. Get out there and play! "Couples who keep sparking well into their golden years have a sense of humor and

playfulness—finding even the idiosyncrasies in each other to be more amusing than maddening."

♥ 10 Ways to Offer Unexpected Encouragement

1. Listen, so you know where encouragement is needed.

2. Believe in his abilities and tell him so.

3. Gather information about classes on a subject he finds particularly interesting. Sign him up for this class, schedule permitting.

4. Mail a card to his office thanking him for the energy and expertise he exhibits as he works to help provide for your family.

5. Notice and comment on his good points.

6. Plan surprises. This can be simple, like his favorite candy bar, to whatever extravagance your family spending plan allows.

7. Tuck a love note in his briefcase, suitcase, or pillowcase so he knows you are thinking about him.

8. Celebrate him! This celebration need not be a birthday event. Make it an unexpected time to help him know that he is appreciated. (Maybe even roll out a red carpet.)

9. Make a "Yeah, Dad!" video as a family encouragement video production. Interview your children and ask them to talk about what makes their father special. Be creative and include props, music, and anything else

that Dad would love. Prepare popcorn and watch the video as a family.

10. Do a "Children's Choice Award" ceremony and present Dad with a homemade, child-designed award. Inscribe: "To a One-in-a-Million Dad" on a gold plate and affix it to the base of the award.

Here is a good recipe for award making:

1½ **cups salt**
4 **cups flour**
1½ **cups water**
1 **teaspoon alum**

Mix the dry ingredients together in a plastic bowl, then add water gradually. When dough forms a ball around the spoon, knead the dough well, adding water if it is too crumbly.

This clay can also be baked. Set the oven to 300° and bake small shapes for 30–40 minutes or until hard.

💜 5 Ways to Offer Significant Support to Your Husband

I asked a close friend of our family's, Shirley Crouch, a mother of two, how she always seemed to be so supportive of her husband's political career. She shared the following ideas:

1. By praying for him. I give everything that he does to the Lord. I continually pray for his day, his relationships at work, his witness, and his protection.

2. By taking care of our home and children. The primary ministry God has given me is attending to the daily needs of our children and our home. I do this as unto the Lord because I know that this relieves Jim of that stress.

3. By being willing to support him in his job. This might be as simple as attending political events with him or being involved as his campaign manager or treasurer. The more politically active I am, the stronger our team becomes.

4. By listening to him. Communication is a key to every marriage, but the idea of listening to your husband to find out his needs is of high importance.

5. By sharing my insights with him. It is not that I am simply giving my advice or opinion in every situation, but I know that I truly support him when I can offer him my wisdom. I occasionally have to be a voice of reason and graciously say no when one more commitment might not be good for our family.

*There is no spectacle on earth more appealing
than that of a beautiful woman cooking dinner
for someone she loves.*

Thomas Wolfe

♥ 5 Great Make-Ahead Meals He Will Love

Freezer Teasers

Frozen foods are best when they are wrapped and stored properly. Here are some helpful suggestions for storing your meals:

- ♥ Cool foods first. Let foods cool to room temperature before freezing. This way the dish will freeze faster and will not raise the temperature of your freezer.

- ♥ No guessing here: Before freezing, label each package with the name of the dish, the date prepared, and defrosting and cooking instructions. This helps if the recipe is lost or if you take this dish to someone that will not have the recipe. If using aluminum foil, you can write directly onto the foil with a permanent marker.

- ♥ Think before you thaw. Thaw frozen foods left in foil in the refrigerator on a tray. Some dishes can be defrosted in the microwave. Thawing foods at room temperature may promote spoilage and bacteria growth.

Recipes

Three-Cheese Baked Potatoes

Things You'll Need:

knife

spoon
medium mixing bowl
grater
measuring cups
measuring spoons
electric mixer
foil
freezer bag
cookie sheet

Ingredients:

4 medium baking potatoes
vegetable oil
½ cup sour cream
¼ cup milk or half-and-half
¼ cup butter
⅛ cup Cheddar cheese, shredded
⅛ cup Parmesan cheese, shredded
⅛ cup blue cheese, crumbled (substitute Edam cheese if preferred)
½ teaspoon salt
¼ teaspoon pepper
Optional: cooked and crumbled bacon, ¼ cup chopped chives

Directions:

1. Wash potatoes and rub the skins with oil. Bake at 400° for one hour.

2. Remove from oven and let cool thoroughly.

3. Cut a 1½-inch strip lengthwise on the top of each potato and carefully scoop out the pulp so the skin will stay intact.

4. In a medium mixing bowl combine potato pulp and the remaining ingredients.

5. Beat with a mixer until light and fluffy; fill shells with mixture.

To Freeze:

Wrap each potato in aluminum foil. Place in a reclosable plastic freezer bag and place in the freezer.

To Reheat:

When ready to cook, remove from freezer and defrost at room temperature for 20 minutes. Preheat the oven to 400°. Place the foil-wrapped potatoes onto a cookie sheet and into the oven. Bake for 20 minutes or until warmed through.

❤ ❤ ❤

Recipes

Fresh Tomato Corn and Pasta Pie

Things You'll Need:

10-inch deep-dish pie plate

measuring cups
measuring spoons
grater
knife
medium bowl
spoon

Ingredients:

6 ounces packaged spaghetti
2 tablespoons butter
⅓ cup Parmesan cheese, grated
2 eggs
2 cups tomatoes, chopped
1 cup corn
½ cup carrot, shredded
⅓ cup onion, chopped
¾ teaspoon dried oregano
1 clove garlic, finely chopped

Directions:

1. Cook pasta according to package directions, drain.

2. Stir butter and Parmesan cheese into the pasta. Cool.

3. Add eggs and stir well.

4. Place pasta mixture in the 10-inch pie plate. Use the back of a spoon to shape pasta into a pie shell. Bake at 350° for 8 minutes or until set.

5. In a medium bowl combine the remaining ingredients. Pour into pasta pie shell and bake for 20 minutes.

To Freeze:

Wrap the pie tightly with aluminum foil. Place in a reclosable freezer bag.

Write the date on a piece of masking tape and place on the freezer bag.

To Reheat:

When ready to bake, preheat the oven to 350° and bake for 30 minutes or until warmed through.

❤   ❤   ❤

Recipes

Sweet and Sour Meatloaf with Chive Polenta

Things You'll Need:

food processor
measuring cups
measuring spoons
spoon
large mixing bowl
small bowl
wire rack
jelly roll pan

Ingredients:

3 slices wheat bread

½ cup medium yellow onion, peeled and roughly
   chopped
2 cloves garlic, peeled and chopped
½ cup ketchup
2 teaspoons dry mustard
1½ pounds ground round beef
2 large eggs, beaten
2 teaspoons salt
1 teaspoon pepper
1 teaspoon Tabasco

Sauce:

3 tablespoons ketchup
2 tablespoons brown sugar
2½ teaspoons dried mustard

Directions:

1. Preheat the oven to 400°, remove the crust from the bread.

2. Process the bread in a food processor until fine. Place bread crumbs in a large mixing bowl.

3. Add onion to the food processor and process until fine. Add to the bread crumbs.

4. Add garlic, ketchup, mustard, ground round, eggs, and seasonings to mixing bowl. Knead together with hands until thoroughly mixed.

5. Using your hands, form an elongated loaf. Place meatloaf on a wire rack and onto a jelly roll pan (a cookie sheet with sides).

6. In a small bowl combine the sauce ingredients and stir thoroughly. Using a pastry brush, brush the top of the meatloaf with the sauce.

7. Bake for about 35 minutes or until a meat thermometer registers 160°.

To Freeze:

Cool the meatloaf completely and then wrap it tightly with aluminum foil. Place it in a reclosable freezer bag and then into the freezer.

To Reheat:

Defrost for about 30 minutes. Preheat oven to 400°. Place on a cookie sheet and cover with foil. Place in the oven for 20 minutes or until heated through.

♥ ♥ ♥

Recipes

Chive Polenta

Things You'll Need:
measuring cups
measuring spoons
saucepan
knife
spoon

Ingredients:

2 cups water
½ cup milk (add more if needed)
1½ teaspoons salt
1 cup corn kernels
½ cup fresh chives, chopped
2 cups quick-cooking polenta
4 tablespoons butter
½ teaspoon pepper

Directions:

1. In a medium saucepan add water, salt, corn, and milk.

2. Place on high heat and bring to a boil. Slowly pour the polenta into the saucepan, stirring constantly.

3. Reduce the heat to low. Simmer, stirring often, until the polenta is thick, about 6 minutes.

4. Stir in the chives, butter, and pepper.

To Freeze:

Cool. Place in a reclosable freezer bag. Label with recipe name and date.

To Reheat:

Defrost for 30 minutes, add to a medium sauce pan with a little water and milk. Stir until thoroughly heated.

❤ ❤ ❤

Herb Dumpling and Chicken Casserole

Things You'll Need:

medium-sized mixing bowl
measuring cups
measuring spoons
stockpot
spoon
knife
large casserole dish

Ingredients:

2 cups self-rising flour
2 tablespoons fresh or dried herbs, chopped
¾ cup milk
¼ cup oil
6 boneless, skinless chicken breasts
4 cups water, chicken stock, or chicken broth
3 chicken bouillon cubes
½ teaspoon salt
¼ teaspoon pepper
1 small yellow onion, quartered
2 stalks celery broken into pieces

Directions:

1. Place water, chicken stock, or chicken broth into a large stock pan.

2. Add bouillon cubes, seasonings, onion, celery, and herbs. Add chicken and boil until cooked.

3. Mix together the flour, herbs, milk, and oil and roll out onto a floured surface. Cut into 1½-inch strips and cut the strips into 2-inch pieces. Add dumplings to boiling chicken broth. Do not stir. Cook for 20 minutes on medium heat.

4. Add 1 cup milk and 1 stick of butter. Cook until the butter is melted.

5. Pour into a large casserole dish and cool.

To Freeze:

Cover very tightly with plastic wrap and then aluminum foil. Label. Place into a jumbo freezer bag, then into the freezer.

To Reheat:

Defrost for about 30 minutes. Preheat the oven to 400°. Remove plastic wrap and cover with foil. Bake for 20 minutes or until warmed through.

❤   ❤   ❤

Recipes

Peanut Butter Cake with Peanut Butter Cup Ice Cream

Things You'll Need:

medium mixing bowl
measuring cups
measuring spoons
electric mixer
13 x 9 x 2-inch pan

Ingredients:

¾ cup butter, softened
1 cup creamy peanut butter
2 cups firmly packed brown sugar
3 eggs
2 cups all-purpose flour
1 tablespoon baking powder
½ teaspoon salt
1 cup milk
2 teaspoons vanilla

Directions:

1. In a medium mixing bowl, cream together butter and peanut butter; gradually add sugar, beating well at medium speed with an electric mixer.

2. Add eggs, one at a time, and beat well after each addition.

3. Combine flour, baking powder, and salt; add alternately dry ingredients and milk to creamed mixture, beginning and ending with flour mixture. Mix after each addition. Stir in vanilla.

4. Pour the batter into a greased and floured 13 x 9 x 2-inch pan. Bake for 35 to 40 minutes at 350°.

To Freeze:

Wrap tightly with plastic wrap and then with foil. Label. Place into a jumbo freezer bag, then into the freezer.

❤   ❤   ❤

Recipes

Peanut Butter Cup Ice Cream

Things You'll Need:

food processor
knife
plastic container with lid

Ingredients:

1 quart vanilla bean ice cream
1 cup peanut butter cups, roughly chopped

Directions:

1. Place ice cream in a food processor and process until smooth.

2. Add the peanut butter cups and process until combined.

3. Place ice cream in a plastic container with lid and place back into freezer to freeze until firm.

♥ ♥ ♥

Children Matter

- 6 Birthday Party Ideas, Percolating with Pizzazz

- 9 Ways to Bring Your Child's Favorite Books to Life

- 4 Ways to Corral Clutter

- 10 Ways to Create a Space for Imaginations to Soar

- 10 Quick and Cute Teacher Gifts

- 8 Car Games for Adventurous Travelers

- 8 Activities for Your Kids While You Prepare Dinner

- 6 Ways to Make Bible Verse Memory Fun and Exciting

- 5 Ways to Teach Your Child the Art of Sharing

- 7 Ways to Have a Successful Party with Kids

- 7 Ways to Talk to Your Teen

- 12 Things to Pray for Your Children

- 7 Ways to Achieve Summer Sanity

- 5 Frozen Fun Ideas

- 3 Ideas for Adentures with Apples

- 10 Rainy Day Activities

- 🖤 10 Vital Life Skills to Teach Your Child
- 🖤 7 Themed Lunches for the Week
- 🖤 10 Terrific Tips for Tortillas
- 🖤 26 Ways to Say "I Love You"
- 🖤 17 Great Books for Young Children

Children Matter

*I prayed for this child, and the LORD has
granted me what I asked of him.*

1 Samuel 1:27

Henry Ward Beecher said that a mother's heart is a child's classroom. Is that not a riveting thought? Our hearts govern who we are and what our children may become. A mother's heart must constantly follow a priority checklist to direct each aspect of life. We must establish correct heart attitudes before trying to lead our little ones toward God. We are supposed to do this between the nurturing, laundry, ballet lessons, grocery shopping, PTA meetings, church activities, and so on. In conjunction with all our other tasks, we are bringing home the bacon, frying it up in a pan, and not ever letting our husband forget he's a man. Whew! It makes me tired just thinking about it.

Motherhood is a juggling act, albeit one well worth the effort, especially when your eyes meet the eyes of the small person God entrusted to your care. Those eyes reflect the glow and sparkle of a pure, moldable heart, poised for that next round of rapid-fire questions. "Mommy, does God like my manners today?" "Hey, God," as she is looking towards the sky, "did you see that jump?"

"Will I be growed up by Christmas?" These are just three of the millions of questions our four-year-old daughter, Sarah, asks on a daily basis.

Children are truly a fountain of gladness, a refreshment like no other. A child's creative mind pours out endless comments filled with honesty and joy. Eyes that dance, imaginations that soar, and energy that abounds are only a few characteristics that define the child. I suppose this is why God said, "Behold, children are a gift of the LORD; the fruit of the womb is a reward. Like arrows in the hand of a warrior, so are the children of one's youth. How blessed is the man whose quiver is full of them…" (Psalm 127:3-5).

Shortly after our wedding, I became pregnant. We were shocked, scared, and surprised. Excitement abounded as we debated whether it was a boy or girl, discussed names, and decorated the nursery in our heads. We were moving full force into marriage and parenthood. About 13 weeks into the pregnancy, we again were shocked, scared, and this time petrified. My body definitely was pregnant, there was an amniotic sack for a baby, but no heartbeat, no baby. I had never heard of the condition known as a blighted ovum. I did not care what it was called; it seemed like one of the worst practical jokes one could experience. Fortunately, we found comfort knowing that God was in control. We saw His provision, we felt His peace, and we moved on.

Three years later we became pregnant again and this time a bona fide baby was growing in me. Let me share that story.

My last few weeks of pregnancy brought feelings of uncertainty and excitement. As the clock ticked closer to full-fledged motherhood, fear began to set in. Exactly what did I (and do I now) know about being a mother? Those thoughts would ebb and flow between nursery preparation, baby showers, and doctor appointments. They rushed back like an avalanche as Mark and I packed to leave the hospital. A scant 21 hours after I delivered our child, I was being wheeled out of the hospital over-whelmed with responsibility. This fragile, tiny baby girl was coming home with us to stay.

Two days after Sarah's birth, I found myself walking back into the hospital experiencing physical pain and emotional failure. I was visiting a breast-feeding spe-cialist, a true Mother Earth who would have done quite well as a pioneer woman. When I tried to explain the pain I felt when breast-feeding, she ignored me, (empathy not being her strong suit—breast milk was). Even with the pain, to my surprise, I experienced strong feelings of determination to nurture and feed my baby. (It was a glimmer of pioneer spirit in my modern existence.) You see, I was responsible for this little miracle. I was, and always will be, her mother. The me that once was had been left somewhere on the delivery room floor, probably still embarrassed about being in the stirrups while the world passed by. I felt as though I had Sarah on the 50-yard line during the Super Bowl.

Nursing your baby is supposed to be natural and best for baby's health, not to mention mom's weight loss. I signed up thinking what a great deal it was—no bottles to wash and warm nourishment provided free of charge and readily available. What could be simpler? Plenty of things! To begin with, I was utterly (no pun intended) amazed at the whole process. It was astonishing to find milk flowing from my body, almost as strange as if I had found chocolate chips growing between my toes. Is mine the blessed response to motherhood? Probably not, but Norman Rockwell never depicted it this way.

I no longer knew my body and did not recognize my new self-sacrificing, nonsleeping persona. Uninterrupted rest had become part of the past, along with quiet conversation during meals and a peaceful cup of coffee with *Good Morning America.* Replacing my former way of life were puffy eyes, forgetfulness, and even longer to-do lists with no time to do them. Taking care of the baby was the major part of our existence, and I do mean *our.* Mark was a huge support and became quite the diaper-and-outfit-change aficionado.

All I knew was that I was completely and wonderfully in love with my incredibly fascinating baby girl. To be honest, we expected a little blob of clay that would simply lie there for six months and then develop a personality. Wrong again! Our Sarah was an ever-changing bundle of movement, facial expressions, and delightful sounds. With a death grip that could cut off circulation and a whole repertoire of crying melodies, she communicated quite effectively from the beginning.

Her vibrant and expressive personality forced me to realize that we were dealing with a real person, a child of God, entrusted to us for physical and spiritual development.

I know you too have your stories, your feelings of overwhelming joy, and your hopes and dreams of doing the "parent thing" to the glory of God. It is a responsibility like no other…and a gift to you. Our gift back to God is how we grow these little hearts. Parenting is supposed to be a fun ride, so fasten your seatbelt and choose to make it a good one.

Party Planners

♥ 6 Birthday Party Ideas, Percolating with Pizzazz

Great parties are not so much doing something spectacular. Parties with pizzazz are about presentation and a welcoming environment.

1. Polka-Dot Party

Invitations—Polka dots are whimsical, fanciful, and fun little circles that are a true sprinkling of spring. Purchase colored notecards (most card stores sell paper by the pound). Using a hole punch, punch out holes around the perimeter of the card. Write your party invitation on the "polka-dot" card. Save the holes, because they will double as polka dots.

Decorations—Purchase some adhesive dots at an office supply store. Stick them to the entryway of your home, on a white sheet to use for a tablecloth, or on sweatshirts for the polka-dot theme. Also, unravel some white sewing thread and stick two stickers (sticky sides together, color facing out) back to back with the thread in between. This makes a polka-dot garland perfect for decorating a light fixture.

Food—Small pastel mints work great stuck into the icing on a cake. Also try M&M's on cupcakes, gumdrops on cookies, and chocolate chips sprinkled on ice cream.

2. Candy Crazy

Invitations—On a small mailing tube, write the specifics of your party on a piece of white paper. Roll the paper into the mailing tube. Fill the tube with your favorite wrapped candies.

Decorations—Line the sidewalk to your home with wrapped candies. Use a clear vase filled with candy as a centerpiece. Tie a string around a piece of candy, unravel the string about two feet, and cut. Using a thumb tack, tack the long end of the string to the ceiling.

Food—Have an ice cream sundae buffet. Fill small galvanized buckets with colorful candies (M&M's, Sprinkles, Gummy Bears, Skittles, and carob-coated raisins). Fill a larger galvanized bucket with ice cream balls. Let the children create their own flavorful and colorful sundaes.

3. Storybook Silliness

Invitations—Write the invitation in the front pages of a copy of the storybook providing your theme.

Decorations—Say you are creating your party around the book *Where the Wild Things Are* by Maurice Sendak. The decorations could be lots of plants, paper boats, and monster masks. Your party honoree could dress up in a wolf suit, similar to what Max wore in the book.

Food—Here are a few easy recipes that would make fun projects to do at the party:

Recipes

Wild Things Claws

1 can large biscuits
½ stick butter, melted
½ cup sugar
1 teaspoon cinnamon
strawberry preserves
almond slices

1. Place the sugar and cinnamon into a small bowl and stir to combine.

2. Melt the butter and put it in a small bowl.

3. Place each biscuit in the butter and turn to coat. Place the butter-coated biscuit into the cinnamon/sugar mixture and then onto a cookie sheet.

4. Using the back of a tablespoon, make a big indentation in the biscuit and fill the indention with preserves.

5. Place five almond slices per biscuit along one side to represent the wild things' claws.

6. Bake according to package directions.

Recipes

Yellow Eyes

2 vanilla wafers per child
yellow frosting
mini chocolate chips

1. Place the vanilla wafers on paper plates.

2. Frost the wafers with yellow frosting.

3. Place the mini chocolate chips in a circle in the center of the frosted wafer to form the yellow-eye pupil.

4. Glamour Galore

Invitations—Using fabric paint, write your invitations on a white cotton glove. Be sure to paint the glove's "fingernails" and affix sparkly jewels and sequins to dress up the invitation. Save the other glove for an art project during the party.

Decorations—Hats, boas, dress-up shoes, dress-up dresses, and a video of a fashion show would create a festive environment for the party. Provide disposable cameras for the girls to take their own candid shots during the event. These candid shots would make nice surprises in your thank-you notes.

Food—Try stringing your own edible cereal necklaces onto red licorice strings for a tasty accessory.

Recipes

Glamour Hats

1 prepared pound cake
Several colors of tube frosting
Assorted edible candy flowers and decorative candies

1. Slice the pound cake into one-inch slices. Using a large round cookie cutter, cut one circle.

2. Take another one-inch slice of pound cake. Using a smaller round cookie cutter, cut another circle.

3. Center the smaller cake round on top of the larger cake round. Using the tube frosting as "glue," affix the two together. This will form your cake "hat."

4. Decorate the brim of the hat with edible candy flowers and decorative flowers.

❤   ❤   ❤

5. Tea for Tutu

Invitations—Cut paper in the shape of a teapot. Glue netting around the perimeter of the pot. Write your party particulars in the center.

Decorations—Netting and more netting. Drape this stuff everywhere!! Hang ballet slippers or paper ballet slippers cut from construction paper from the ceiling. Sew netting to the bottom of some large T-shirts and ask each girl to wear their "ballet outfit" for the party.

Food—Prepare Ballet Slipper Sandwiches, Pretty Pink Purses, and Pink Powder Puffs.

Recipes

Ballet Slipper Sandwiches

4 slices of banana bread
¼ cup strawberry cream cheese
¼ cup strawberries, sliced

1. Slice the banana bread and cut into the shape of ballet slippers.

2. Spread one side of the bread with cream cheese and top with sliced strawberries.

3. Top with the second slice of banana bread.

❤   ❤   ❤

Recipes

Pretty Pink Purses

1½ cups low-fat ricotta cheese
½ cup almond slices
3 tablespoons whole cranberry sauce
¼ cup powdered sugar
1 egg
¼ teaspoon almond extract
10 frozen phyllo leaves, thawed
½ cup butter, melted

1. Combine cheese, almonds, cranberry sauce, sugar, egg, and extract in a medium bowl; set aside.

2. Brush one phyllo sheet with butter; fold in half crosswise. Again, brush with butter and fold in half lengthwise. Sprinkle with pink sugar (see recipe below).

3. Spoon ¼ cup cheese mixture into the center of the folded phyllo sheet.

4. Gather the ends towards the center, enclosing the cheese mixture and twist.

5. Brush with butter.

6. Sprinkle with pink sugar. Repeat with remaining phyllo sheets and cheese mixture.

7. Place bundles on a baking sheet and bake at 350° for 18 to 20 minutes.

♥   ♥   ♥

Recipes

Pink Sugar

½ cup sugar
1 drop red food coloring

1. In a small bowl mix to combine, cover with plastic wrap
   until ready to use.

♥   ♥   ♥

Recipes

Pink Powder Puffs

1 angel food cake
1 box powdered sugar
¼ stick butter, melted
½ cup milk
½ teaspoon vanilla
1 teaspoon red food coloring

1. Purchase an angel food cake and tear it into pieces.

2. In a medium bowl, place powdered sugar, butter, milk,
   coloring, and vanilla. Stir thoroughly to combine. (Add
   more milk to get proper consistency for dipping.)

3. Dip the torn angel food cake into the icing and place on
   waxed paper to dry.

❤ ❤ ❤

6. Chef's Choice

Invitations—Design your own take-out menu, listing your party activities as if they are menu options. You could write your menu on bordered paper or on a white dinner napkin using fabric paints. Deliver this to your party guests on a silver platter, wearing a chef's hat.

Decorations—Use a vegetable-print tablecloth. Fill galvanized buckets with cooking utensils, cookie cutters, and recipe cards. Provide little stations around your party area: one for making handprints on aprons and one for measuring, stirring, pouring, and "cooking" with dried beans and rice. Another station is for favorite foods—cut out numerous food pictures and ask the children to glue their favorite foods onto a paper plate.

Food—Lavish your little cooks with fun and yummy pudding squares and spicy snowflakes.

Recipes

Fudgy Pudding Squares

1 3⅜-ounce box of chocolate pudding mix (cooked type)
1 box chocolate cake mix
1 (6-ounce) bag semi-sweet chocolate chips
½ cup chopped rainbow sprinkles, optional

1. Prepare pudding mix according to package directions.

2. Blend the dry chocolate cake mix into the pudding; stir to combine.

3. Pour into a greased 9 x 13-inch pan, sprinkle with chocolate chips and sprinkles.

4. Bake at 350° for 30 to 35 minutes.

Recipes

Cinnamon Snowflakes

soft flour tortillas
1 stick butter, melted
½ cup sugar
1 teaspoon cinnamon

1. Fold the flour tortillas into fourths, using kitchen scissors cut triangle shapes into the tortillas. (This is just like making paper snowflakes in grade school.)

2. Combine sugar and cinnamon.

3. Brush tortilla with melted butter and sprinkle with sugar mixture.

4. Bake at 350° for 8 minutes or until golden brown.

♥ ♥ ♥

A home without books is like a room without windows.
A little library, growing every year, is an honorable part of
a man's history. It is a man's duty to have books.
A library is not a luxury, but one of the necessities of life.

Henry Ward Beecher

♥ 9 Ways to Bring Your Child's Favorite Books to Life

Anything to do with reading and writing needs to be fun. Knowing your child's interests and passions will help you develop your own strategies for giving your children a lifelong love of reading.

1. Match art projects to your child's favorite stories. One entertaining example would be *Miss Fannie's Hat* by Jan Karon. To make your own "fancy" hats like Miss Fannie's, purchase an inexpensive straw hat and hot glue silk flowers all over it.

2. Design T-shirts to go with their favorite story.

3. Read *The Very Hungry Caterpillar* by Eric Carle. Purchase a caterpillar and watch it transform into a butterfly. Or order a Butterfly Garden by Insect Lore (about $20.00 through educational toy, novelty, and nature stores), or through the Internet at www.sciencestuff. com or www.liveandlearn.com.

4. Read *How Are You Peeling?* by Saxton Freymann and Joost Elffers. Design your own fruit and vegetable faces and discuss the feelings or emotions behind each face.

5. Act out a story using puppets, friends, and family members. Don't forget your video camera.

6. During the holidays, offer "book specials" in addition to the television specials. Go to the bookstore or library and find stories that match the specific holiday, put on seasonal dress-up clothes, and prepare snacks that tie into the story.

7. Create a special reading spot. An old footed bathtub filled with soft pillows, a big porch swing plump with oversized pillows, a day bed covered with a soft blanket, or a tree house containing an oversized beanbag chair are cozy and inviting places.

8. If your child loves Madeline books, take her adventures to another level. Find travel posters about France and hang them in your reading area, enjoy a tour of Paris via the Internet, or visit a French bakery for cream puffs and eclairs.

9. Cut out pictures of your child's favorite things from different magazines, place the pictures on the table, and let them create a story as they choose pictures from the stack. Write down the story in their own words. Fold several pieces of construction paper and glue the pictures to the paper, cut out the words, and glue to the bottom of the matching picture.

But everything should be done in a fitting and orderly way.

1 Corinthians 14:40 NIV

💜 4 Ways to Corral Clutter

1. Label plastic boxes with lids, just a little larger than a shoe box. These work great for Barbie clothes and shoes, Legos, doll clothes, plastic food, and accumulated crayons.

2. Once a month do a clean sweep, removing items that your children do not play with, like the little toys from fast-food restaurants, etc. If they are in good shape, donate them to a charity or save to fill a piñata for a birthday event.

3. To help with pile control, decide on a drop-off spot for mail, library books, dry cleaning, backpacks, homework, keys, etc.

4. As Emilie Barnes states in her book *Emilie's Creative Home Organizer*, "Sometimes all it takes to eliminate mess, clutter, and confusion are a few hooks here, a basket or two there, and a bit of reshuffling of items on a shelf."

💜 10 Ways to Create a Space for Imaginations to Soar

1. Provide a flat surface for painting.

2. Use a shower curtain for a drop cloth.

3. Use an old door across two wooden boxes for a table.

4. Use old shirts, towels, or pillowcases for smocks.

5. Keep supplies accessible.

6. Use washable surfaces.

7. Keep old towels close by.

8. Designate an area for displaying artwork.

9. Use lazy Susan carousels.

10. Use muffin pans to hold beads, buttons, or paint.

*Love is that condition in which the happiness of
another person is essential to your own joy.*
Robert A. Heinlein

💜 10 Quick and Cute Teacher Gifts

1. Popcorn bowl full of microwave popcorn bags, small sodas, candies, and paid passes to the video store.

2. A big apple cookie jar filled with favorite cookies.

3. Bubble bath and a classical CD.

4. A personalized journal.

5. Unique glass bottles for bubble bath or for dish-washing soap.

6. A glass carafe filled with colorful silk scarves or ties. Add a long straw and top with a white handkerchief so it resembles a sundae.

7. Eight grapevine wreaths large enough to set dinner plates on. These make for interesting place settings.

8. Stocked picnic basket filled with plastic ware and non-perishable foods.

9. A basket filled with magazines of interest. Tuck a subscription into one.

10. A hatbox full of fruit and a fruit smoothie cookbook.

To travel hopefully is a better thing than to arrive.
Robert Lewis Stevenson

♥ 8 Car Games for Adventurous Travelers

1. Create a Stuff Sack—Each child will be responsible for their own "stuff sack." They should choose travel-friendly items and fill their bag with things they like. Another "super stuff sack" would act as the family travel bag. Try items like paper, pencils, maps and

brochures of destinations, songbooks, tapes, and books. Even include equipment for unsightly car sickness: paper lunch sacks, a damp rag, motion illness medicine, and happy traveler stickers.

2. Alphabet Game—Look for letters of the alphabet in consecutive order on road signs, billboards, license plates, and restaurant and gas station signs.

3. Colors of the Rainbow—Look for cars that resemble the colors of the rainbow. To make it more fun, try finding them in the order from top to bottom of God's real and beautiful rainbow: red, orange, yellow, green blue, indigo, and violet.

4. Raindrop Races—If it's raining during your car trip, try watching raindrops on your windows. Find two raindrops at the top of the window and watch them race down to the bottom. Try to guess which one will win!

5. Tell Ongoing Stories—Start the topic as you leave home and spin a tale all the way to your destination. Make it a round-robin story. Let one person start, then go around the car so that each person can add his or her literary points.

6. Chart Your Destinations—Using an atlas, place a star over your final destination. Track your progress from city to city using a highlighter. This might help eliminate the "Are we there yet?" questions.

7. Make a Travel Book—As you travel take pictures of the welcome signs you see entering different states. Next to those pictures write the state capital, flower, bird, and license plate logo. Collect travel literature pertaining to your family's interests. Do your state-by-state or city-by-city travel log as you move from place to place.

8. License Plate Bingo—Make copies of a United States map and give each older child a copy. As you see license plates from different states, mark those states with American flag stickers.

💜 8 Activities for Your Kids While You Prepare Dinner

1. Using colorful electric tape, mark off an indoor hopscotch game. If room allows, place it in the kitchen and watch them play hopscotch while you chop and cook.

2. Erect a tent using a large quilt and some dining room chairs and watch their imaginations soar.

3. Ask your older children to write a story or poem about their day. If they need a little help, give them a brief story introduction sentence that piques their interests and let them "go to town" writing.

4. Write letters or draw pictures to mail to family and friends who live elsewhere.

5. Set up an indoor bowling alley. You will need empty, clean plastic bottles and a kick ball. Line the "pins" up at the end of your hallway. Roll the ball to see how many pins you can knock down.

6. Fill metal mixing bowls with a variety of dried beans, uncooked rice, and corn kernels. Give them all sizes of measuring cups and a clear plastic container. Ask the children to measure the ingredients into the clear plastic container, alternating colors.

7. Set out different colors of Play-Doh, cookie cutters, cookie sheets, muffin pans, and plates. Ask them to create a pretend dinner while you cook. This is a good way to teach food groups and food colors, textures, and tastes.

8. Ask each child to put on their favorite dress-up clothes. Mom and Dad, you too can participate. All you need are hats, gloves, tacky jewelry...

You shall teach them [God's precepts] diligently to your sons [and daughters] and shall talk of them when you sit in your house and when you walk by the way and when you lie down and when you rise up.

Deuteronomy 6:7

♥ 6 Ways to Make Bible Verse Memory Fun and Exciting

1. Make a verse into a cheer. Read *Let's Make a Memory* by Gloria Gaither and Shirley Dobson.

2. Set the verse to music using a familiar tune your children know and love.

3. Create a story that incorporates the true message of the verse, and then act out the story.

4. Ask each family member to choose several favorite verses, write the verses down, including where they appear in the Bible, and place them in a jar. After dinner take turns going around the table, selecting and reading each person's favorite verses.

5. Play hide and seek with scriptures. Write down simple scriptures on colorful cards and hide them around your home. Set a timer and have the children race to find the verses. Once they have all been found, read them together and share what they mean to you. Remind the children that we are to hide God's Word in our heart.

6. Learn scriptures together as a family. Initiate a warm and inviting environment for sharing Bible stories, emphasize why focusing on God's Word is important (so that our lives may be more like Jesus), and have fun doing it.

Practice tenderhearted mercy and kindness to others...
Most of all, let love guide your life.

Colossians 3:12,14 TLB

💜 5 Ways to Teach Your Child the Art of Sharing

1. Always look for ways to include your child in your gift giving and sharing.

2. Brainstorm with your child on ways to make a sad friend smile.

3. Make an action plan for sharing. Prepare an easy and age-appropriate plan so that the child may take an active role.

4. When delivering a gift, take the children with you and make them an important part of the delivery.

5. Be a model for your children by sharing your resources with a family less fortunate, donating clothes or supplies to natural disaster victims, collecting toys for a toy drive, or baking a batch of cookies for a sick neighbor.

💜 7 Ways to Have a Successful Party with Kids

1. Include them in the planning.

2. Give them age-appropriate jobs.

3. Peruse websites for fun ideas.

4. Gather supplies in advance of planned activities.

5. Establish who will be the activity helper adult or teenager.

6. Go over party manners prior to guests' arrival.

7. Have clothes selected and ready.

💜 7 Ways to Talk to Your Teen

Gracie Malone, friend, author, speaker, and mother, wrote an article entitled "Can We Talk, Communicating With Your Teen." In it she offers several ways we as parents can have meaningful conversations with our teenage children:

1. Encourage expression.

2. Learn to say "I'm sorry."

3. Take time to talk.

4. Be available.

5. Just listen. "He who answers before listening—that is his folly and his shame" (Proverbs 18:13 NIV).

6. A well-proven parent-teen communication principle: Teens talk best after dark, in the car, away from home, and with food.

7. Sometimes it is best to depart from parental wisdom and empathize.

Do not be anxious about anything, but in everything,
by prayer and petition, with thanksgiving,
present your requests to God. And the peace of God,
which transcends all understanding,
will guard your hearts and your minds in Christ Jesus.

Philippians 4:6,7 NIV

💜 12 Things to Pray for Your Children

1. That they will know Christ as Savior early in life.

2. That they will have a hatred for sin.

3. That they will be caught when guilty.

4. That they will be protected from the evil one in each area of their lives: spiritual, emotional, and physical.

5. That they will have a responsible attitude in all their interpersonal relationships.

6. That they will respect those in authority over them.

7. That they will desire the right kinds of friends.

8. That they will be kept from the wrong mate and saved for the right one.

9. That they, as well as those they marry, will be kept pure until marriage.

10. That they will learn to totally submit to God and actively resist Satan in all circumstances.

11. That they will be singlehearted, willing to be sold out to Jesus Christ.

12. That they will be hedged in so they cannot find their way to wrong people or wrong places and that the wrong people cannot find their way to them.

Moms and Daughters: Becoming Friends

Susie Hawkins is a wife and the mother of two grown daughters. She is a Bible teacher and speaker and a contributor to *Shine* magazine. (Though Susie has girls, her words of wisdom can provide insight into the mother-son relationship as well.)

What is your goal for your relationship with your daughter? So much of our time and energy is spent during the child-rearing years in "mothering." However, before you know it, your daughter is grown and on her own. What will your relationship be like when your daily mothering is no longer required? First of all, you are always a mother! Even though adult children make their own decisions, there are always times when they just need mom! Yet the relationship does change...and it is wise to realize this during their growing-up years and to prepare for it. If your goal is to develop a strong,

vibrant friendship (which is incredibly rewarding), then the suggestions below may help you.
They also should encourage you as you relate to
your own mother as a friend.

Respect. Look at your daughter with respect as a
person, not just your little girl. She may have different dreams than you did, different gifts, and
different ways of expressing herself. Give her
some space (within reasonable limitations!) to
be who she is. Try to see your child not just with
the identity as "my daughter," but a future adult
with something to contribute to our world.

Mutual Interests. Finding mutual interests can
also be helpful in strengthening the mother-
daughter relationship. An activity that both of
you enjoy will give you great pleasure and be a
special time that you both share well into the
adult years.

Kind Gestures. Find something specific you can
do for your daughter (or mom) that would be
especially meaningful to her, something out of
the ordinary. Perhaps you could ask her, "How
can I pray for you this week?" or "Is there anything I can do for you today?" A little extra
thoughtfulness goes a long way in improving
relationships.

♥ 7 Ways to Achieve Summer Sanity

1. 1,2,3, Draw! Try some water gun fun. Stretch out a big roll of butcher paper, place some blobs of paint on the paper and spray with water guns. Watch the colors run, fade, and shade into great shapes and sizes.

2. Fancy Glasses. Purchase some plastic sunglasses and push out the lenses. You will need feathers, beads, buttons, bows, and glue. Decorate the glasses in fun and imaginative ways.

3. Smoothie Woothies. Place 1 cup vanilla yogurt, ½ cup orange juice, and ½ cup sliced strawberries into a blender and puree until smooth.

4. Wild and Wacky T-shirts. Take a simple white shirt and rubber band off different sections, then dip in colorful dye. Dry. Undo the rubber bands, thoroughly dry. Use this as a swimsuit cover-up.

5. Water Hose Dodge. Put on those swimsuits, fire up that hose, and dodge the sprayer. A real-fun-in-the-sun adventure.

6. Hide from the Heat. Pull out the board games when the heat is really on. Take a quiet break under a ceiling fan and play.

7. Entrepreneurial Kids. The older kids might want to try to invent or establish their own business.

💜 5 Frozen Fun Ideas

Summertime and frozen treats go hand in hand. The most exciting summer sound to a child is the melodious bells of the famous ice cream truck as they round the corner and head for your street.

Snow cones and chocolate fudge bars add sweet flavors to an extra hot day. The frozen fun also adds an air conditioning from the inside out and (if eaten too fast) a real brain freeze.

It is easy to keep the frozen section of your refrigerator packed with make-ahead ice cream treats.

When summer is sizzling, don't wait for the ice cream truck's song. Start your own music and make your favorite chillers with these simple and satisfying sensations.

Recipes

Big Fat Ice Cream Sandwiches

Ingredients:

1 package (18.5 ounces) chocolate cake mix
½ cup water
2 eggs
your favorite ice cream

Directions:

1. Preheat oven to 375°. Spray cookie sheet with cooking spray.

2. Mix together cake mix, water, and eggs.

3. Drop the dough by rounded tablespoonfuls three inches apart onto the prepared cookie sheet.

4. Bake for 6 to 8 minutes or until almost no impression remains when the cookie is touched lightly.

5. Cool the cookies on a cookie sheet; then place on a cooling rack with a spatula.

6. After the cookies have cooled completely, turn one cookie upside down and put a small scoop of ice cream on the flat side. Spread the ice cream around with the back of the spoon.

7. Place the flat side of a second cookie on the ice cream. Wrap the sandwich in plastic wrap and place it in the freezer until the ice cream hardens.

❤   ❤   ❤

Recipes

Quick Fruit Sorbet

Ingredients:

1 large can fruit, packed in heavy syrup (apricots, cherries, tropical mixed fruit)

Directions:

1. Freeze the can of fruit.

2. Cut both ends of the can out and slide the frozen fruit into a food processor.

3. Process until smooth.

4. Pour into glass loaf pans and refreeze. Serve with shortbread cookies.

Recipes

Frozen Chocolate Cream

Ingredients:
1 tablespoon powdered sugar
¼ cup cocoa
2 cups whipping cream
1 teaspoon vanilla extract

Directions:

1. In a small bowl, sift together the powdered sugar and cocoa.

2. Pour the whipping cream into a larger bowl and stir in vanilla. Beat with an electric mixer until thick.

3. Spoon the chocolate mixture into the cream a little at a time and beat until soft peaks form.

4. Spoon the mixture into small bowls and place in the freezer until firm.

❤   ❤   ❤

Recipes

Frozen Fruit Bites

Ingredients:

1½ cups strawberries, finely chopped
½ cup raspberries
1 (8-ounce) can pineapple in syrup, drained
1 peach, peeled and finely chopped
½ cup mini marshmallows
1 cup frozen whipped topping, thawed
1 (12-ounce) box vanilla wafers

Directions:

1. Combine strawberries, raspberries, pineapple, peach, and marshmallows in a blender; blend thoroughly.

2. Fold in the whipped topping.

3. Spoon about 1 tablespoon of the fruit mixture on the flat side of the wafer. Top with the flat side of the second wafer; repeat with remaining wafers.

4. Cover and freeze until firm.

❤   ❤   ❤

Recipes

Cool Banana Pops

Ingredients:

6 bananas
½ cup creamy peanut butter
1 cup carob chips (or Chocolate morsels)
Popsicle sticks

Directions:

1. Peel bananas. Cut each in half crosswise and insert a Popsicle stick into each half.

2. With a knife, spread a thin layer of peanut butter over each banana half.

3. Place the bananas on a plate that has been covered with wax paper.

4. Place carob chips in a soup bowl or shallow bowl.

5. Roll the peanut butter bananas in the carob chips.

6. Place bananas in the freezer for at least 1 to 2 hours. Serve frozen.

❤   ❤   ❤

♥ 3 Ideas for Adventures with Apples

Autumn is as crisp as the crunch of an apple. Autumn is apple season. When apples are plentiful at the grocer's and harvest baskets have taken over the farmers' markets, you do not have to live near an orchard to pick a wonderful variety of crunchy juicy apples.

Take an apple-picking adventure with your children and try to discover how many varieties of apples are available in your area. The following list is not exclusive, but you might want to use it as a checklist in your apple adventure.

Common Varieties

Golden Delicious—A dessert apple, yellow and sweet; an all-purpose variety.

Red Delicious—A dessert apple, red to burgundy, sweet, crunchy, good for salads, snacks, and eating raw.

Pippin—A dessert apple.

Rome—A cooking apple, tart and red.

Stayman—A baking apple.

Granny Smith—Green, very tart, good for snacks and cooking.

Macintosh—Red, juicy, slightly tart, great for eating and making sauces but not for cooking.

Jonathan—An all-purpose variety.

Winesap—An all-purpose apple, red, tart, good as a snack, raw, cooked, or baked.

Try a taste test using your pick of the different varieties. Prepare a scoring sheet with your children and friends just to see what variety tastes the best to your harvest helpers.

Recipes

Easy Apple Dumplings

Ingredients:

4 large apples
1 package prepared pie dough
½ cup brown sugar
1 teaspoon cinnamon
4 tablespoons butter
1 egg yolk with 1 teaspoon of water

Directions:

1. Wash and core apples.

2. In a small bowl mix together brown sugar and cinnamon. Stuff the mixture into the center of each apple.

3. Set an apple on a square of already prepared pie dough, brush all four sides with a mixture of egg yolk and water. Bring all four edges of the pie dough to the top of the apple. Repeat with the other 3 apples.

4. Bake according to pie dough directions.

❤　❤　❤

Recipes

Apple Butter

Ingredients:

4 quarts apples
2 quarts water
1½ quarts cider
1½ pounds sugar
1 teaspoon cinnamon
1 teaspoon allspice
1 teaspoon cloves

Directions:

1. Wash and peel apples, slice into small bits. Cover with water and boil until soft.

2. Press through a sieve to remove seeds and any hard spots.

3. Bring cider to a boil, add apple pulp and sugar and cook until thickened, stirring constantly to prevent scorching.

4. Add spices and cook 20 minutes.

5. Fill sterilized quart jars and seal.

Your children can decorate the jars and select material to use to cover the tops of the jars. Also, decorate a plain white sticker to label your Apple Butter.

❤   ❤   ❤

Apple Brownies

Ingredients:

1 stick melted butter or margarine

2 eggs

1 cup white sugar

1 cup brown sugar

2 cups flour

2 cups apples, peeled and chopped

2 teaspoons cinnamon

Directions:

1. Mix all ingredients together. Pour into a greased brownie pan. Bake at 350° for about 30 minutes. Serve with a caramel topping or caramel ice cream.

🖤 10 Rainy Day Activities

1. Make a vacation scrapbook. Use everything from your trip: menus, placemats colored at a fast-food restaurant, ticket stubs, brochures, postcards, and pictures.

2. Plan a themed party. Make a guest list, plan the refreshments and decorations, select games or activities for the guests, and make invitations.

3. Do something kind for someone else. You could bake cookies for your local police station or senior citizens home.

4. Prepare pretty packages. Design shoe boxes with cheerful patterns to help store and deliver your cookie surprises.

5. Personalize the switch plates in your children's rooms. Cut a square of fabric, embroidery, old blanket, old dress, or wrapping paper slightly bigger than the switch plate. Glue the fabric to the switch plate and seal it with an acrylic sealer.

6. Make a blessings blanket. Purchase a solid-colored blanket and some fabric paints. Decorate the perimeter of the blanket with the colored fabric paints. Before bedtime each night write your blessing of the day on the blanket, then cover your child with their blessing blanket. Be sure to use this opportunity to remind them of God's love and blessings.

7. Create a scripture memory file box. Decorate a recipe box with beads, bows, stickers, and stars. Write memory verses on index cards and file them in their very own stylish box.

8. Make a family treasure box. Write down the different things you treasure about each family member, throughout the year. Bring out your treasure box at Thanksgiving and look at all you have to be thankful for.

9. Draw a huge "Welcome Home" message with sidewalk chalk for Mom or Dad in your garage.

10. Pull together prop boxes for play. Gather ordinary things in your house to make these boxes according to play themes. *Chef and restaurant*—gather cookie cutters, playdough, bowls, spoons, and menus. *Castle and princess*—gather jewels, castle-making materials, tiaras, clothes, and stick horses. Plan and prop your playtime together.

10 Vital Life Skills to Teach Your Child

1. Have faith in God.

2. Live a healthy lifestyle.

3. Accept failure.

4. Learn self-control.

5. Manage money wisely.

6. Love life.

7. Develop many interests.

8. Appreciate the value of work.

9. Express your anger and grief.

10. Be a good friend.

Marvelous Menus

♥ 7 Themed Lunches for the Week

1. I'm Stuffed

Twice baked potato stuffed with ham and cheese
Celery sticks stuffed with peanut butter
Cream stuffed cupcakes
Juice box

2. Pizza Party Lunch

Pizza pita pocket
Salad pocket with dressing
Pizza crust dessert
Bottled water

3. Awesome Autumn Lunch

Pumpkin bread sandwich
Apple slices with caramel dip
Popcorn with dried fruits
Milk

4. Wild and Woolly Lunch

Claw Sandwiches
Monster Munch

Yellow Eyes
Jungle Juice

Yellow Eyes

2 vanilla wafers per activity
yellow frosting
mini chocolate chips

1. Place the vanilla wafers on the paper plates.

2. Frost the wafers with yellow frosting.

3. Place the mini chocolate chips in a circle in the center of the frosted wafer to form the yellow-eye pupil.

❤   ❤   ❤

5. Holiday Hugs Lunch

Christmas wreath sandwiches
Christmas tree tortilla chips
Strawberry-and-kiwi salad
Chocolate dipped sprinkle pretzels
Hot cocoa

Christmas Wreath Sandwiches

4 slices favorite bread
Peanut butter
Cranberry chutney

1. Place the slices of bread on a cutting board, cut large round circles.

2. Using a smaller round cookie cutter, cut out the center of the bread round.

3. Spread a thick layer of peanut butter topped with a thin layer of cranberry chutney.

❤   ❤   ❤

Christmas Tree Tortilla Chips

6 large tortillas
½ stick butter, melted
½ cup sugar
1 teaspoon cinnamon

1. Cut tortillas using a Christmas tree-shaped cookie cutter.

2. Using a pasty brush, paint melted butter over the cut tortillas.

3. Combine sugar and cinnamon in a small bowl and sprinkle over the butter-covered Christmas tree shapes.

4. Bake at 350° for 8 to 10 minutes.

❤   ❤   ❤

6. Gone Fish'n Lunch

Fish'n pole snack
Goldfish
Fish bait fruit
Gummy worms
Lake water juice

Recipes

Fish'n Pole Snack

pretzel rods
peanut butter
goldfish crackers

Dip the pretzel rods into the peanut butter and pick up a goldfish with your peanut butter-coated "fish'n rod."

❤ ❤ ❤

7. "A" You're Adorable

Alligator Pie (ham pocket)
"A"-shaped bread stick
Apple wedges with peanut butter dip
Alphabet cereal snack

Recipes

Alphabet Cereal Snack

2 cups alphabet cereal
½ cup mini marshmallows
½ cup golden raisins
¼ cup carob chips

Pour all ingredients into a resealable plastic bag and shake to combine.

❤ ❤ ❤

♥ 10 Terrific Tips for Tortillas

The tortilla is a thin round "pancake" full of versatility. Varied sizes, flavors, and textures give the tortilla its proud place of honor in kitchens around the world.

1. **Tortilla Cups.** Place six custard cups on a cookie sheet. Spray around the custard cups with a cooking spray so the overlap of the tortilla will not stick to the pan. Brush a 6-inch flour tortilla with melted butter, place over the custard cup and bake at 350° for 6 to 8 minutes or until browned. Cool. Fill the tortilla cup with scrambled eggs topped with bacon or chicken salad topped with crushed tortilla chips. You can also layer the tortilla cups with taco meat, rice, and lettuce and then top with shredded cheese and tomatoes.

2. **Tortilla Cookies.** Cut a 10-inch flour tortilla with your favorite cookie cutters. Place the shapes on a cookie sheet that has been sprayed with cooking spray. Brush the tortillas with melted butter and sprinkle with cinnamon and sugar. Bake at 350° for 8 to 10 minutes or until golden brown.

3. **Tortilla Club Sandwiches.** Place a 10-inch spinach tortilla on a piece of waxed paper. Spread a thin layer of refried beans on the tortilla and sprinkle with cheese. Place a second tortilla on top, sprinkle with shredded chicken and chopped green onions; place another tortilla on top of the stack. Mix 1 tablespoon of salsa with two tablespoons of sour cream, spread over the tortilla. Sprinkle a layer of shredded lettuce,

cooked and crumbled bacon, and chopped tomato. Top with the last tortilla. Cut into wedges and serve.

4. **Tortilla Lasagna.** Place a layer of sun-dried tomato tortillas on the bottom of a 13 x 9-inch glass baking dish. Top with cooked ground turkey. Layer with flour tortillas and top with fresh or canned tomato sauce. Add a layer of ricotta cheese, green chilies, and cilantro. Add a layer of spinach tortillas. Continue alternating layers until your baking dish is full. Top with tomato sauce and shredded cheese. Bake at 350° for 20 to 25 minutes.

5. **Tortilla Dumplings.** Place 8 (8-inch) corn tortillas on a cutting board and cut into ½-inch strips. Chop a small onion and sauté it with garlic in 2 tablespoons of oil. Add 3 cups of chicken broth, 1 can chopped green chilies, and 2 cans of chunk-style chicken. Add cumin and chili pepper to taste and bring to a boil. Cover, reduce heat and simmer 15 minutes. Add tortillas and 1 to 2 cups of Velveeta cheese. Simmer until the cheese melts. Serve.

6. **Tortilla Crisps.** Place several flavors of 8-inch tortillas on a cutting board, cut into fourths, spray with a butter-flavored cooking spray, and top with shredded Parmesan cheese and sesame seeds. Cut in wedges and bake at 400° for 10 to 12 minutes or until crisp.

7. **Tortilla Pie Crusts.** Spray a 9-inch pie plate with cooking spray. Place 4 (8-inch) tortillas in the pie plate, adjusting them evenly so that the tortillas come

up onto the sides of the pie plate. Set your oven to 400° and bake for 5 minutes. Remove the tortillas from the oven and layer with shredded chicken, corn, salsa, green chilies, corn, crushed tortillas, and shredded cheese. Place into the oven for 10 minutes to warm through.

8. **Tortilla Rolls.** Spread an 8-inch tortilla with strawberry cream cheese, then sprinkle with chopped strawberries and mini chocolate chips. Roll tightly. Place on a cutting board and slice into ½-inch slices.

9. **Fruited Nachos.** Cut 8-inch tortillas into fourths. Brush each tortilla with melted butter and sprinkle heavily with cinnamon and sugar. Bake at 400° until crisp. Make a fruit salsa by chopping a variety of your favorite fruit, then adding 1 teaspoon of chopped mint and a splash of your favorite fruit juice. Place a dollop of fruit salsa on top of each cinnamon crisp nacho. Top with sour cream.

10. **Tortilla Tarts.** Place a 10-inch flour tortilla on a cutting board. Brush a thin layer of caramel sauce over the tortilla. Add thinly cut slices of apple, raisins, and crushed walnuts. Top with a tortilla. Brush with melted butter and sprinkle with a mixture of sugar, ginger, and nutmeg. Bake at 400° for 5 minutes or until warmed through. Remove from oven, cut into fourths, and serve with a caramel dipping sauce.

💜 26 Ways to Say "I Love You"

A is for:

A is for my Amazement with your Angelic Attitude.

> *Have this attitude in yourselves*
> *which was also in Christ Jesus*
> Philippians 2:5

B is for:

B is for your Believable Beauty both inside and out.

> *Be beautiful in your heart by being gentle and quiet.*
> *This kind of beauty will last, and God considers it very special.*
> 1 Peter 3:3,4 CEV

C is for:

C is for your Charming Countenance.

> *I shall yet praise Him, the help of my countenance.*
> Psalm 42:11

D is for:

D is for your Doing of good Deeds.

> *Remind them…to be ready for every good deed.*
> Titus 3:1

E is for:

E is for your Excellence in Everything you do.

If there is any excellence and if anything worthy of praise,
let your mind dwell on these things.
Philippians 4:8

F is for:

F is for your Fancy Faith, a Family treasure to adore.

Now faith is the assurance of things hoped for,
the conviction of things not seen.
Hebrews 11:1

G is for:

G is for God's Goodness in Giving us you.

Children are a gift of the LORD.
Psalm 127:3

H is for:

H is for your Happy Heart and Helpful Hands.

A happy heart makes the face cheerful.
Proverbs 15:13 NIV

I is for:

I is for your Importance in our family and how God will do the Impossible through you.

With men this is impossible,
but with God all things are possible.
Matthew 19:26

J is for:

J is for the Joy you bring just being you.

A joyful heart is good medicine.
Proverbs 17:22

K is for:

K is for the Kindness you show each and every day.

Be kind to one another.
Ephesians 4:32

L is for:

L is for the Love of Laughter you bring to Lighten our Load.

Our mouth was filled with laughter.
Psalm 126:2

M is for:

M is for the many Moments of Music you bring to our hearts.

> *I will sing and make music with all my soul.*
> Psalms 108:1 NIV

N is for:

N is for the Nice Nature you share with Neighbors.

> *Love your neighbor as yourself.*
> Leviticus 19:18

O is for:

O is for being an Obedient, One and Only you.

> *Children, be obedient to your parents in all things,*
> *for this is well-pleasing to the Lord.*
> Colossians 3:20

P is for:

P is for the Pleasing Person you are Practicing to be.

> *We keep His commandments and*
> *do the things that are pleasing in His sight.*
> 1 John 3:22

Q is for:

Q is for your fascinating Qualities and Quick yet Quiet spirit.

In quietness and trust is your strength.
Isaiah 30:15

R is for:

R is for the way you show Respect for the Rules.

If anyone competes as an athlete, he does not win the prize unless he competes according to the rules.
2 Timothy 2:5

S is for:

S is for your Super Smile and Sensational Shine.

Let your light shine before men in such a way that they may see your good works, and glorify your Father who is in heaven.
Matthew 5:16

T is for:

T is for your Terrific Timing in Telling us the Truth.

Speaking the truth in love,
we are to grow up in all aspects into Him.
Ephesians 4:15

U is for:

U is for your Uniqueness Understood by all.

> *I am fearfully and wonderfully made.*
> Psalm 139:14

V is for:

V is for your great Value, a Victory to see.

> *How much more valuable you are than the birds.*
> Luke 12:24

W is for:

W is for your Wonderful Worth, a blessing to this World.

> *You are honored and I love you.*
> Isaiah 43:4

X is for:

X is for how your eXample meets our eXpectations.

> *I gave you an example that you should do as I did to you.*
> John 13:15

Y is for:

Y is for Young You, a job no one can do but YOU.

For I am confident of this very thing, that He who began a good work in you will perfect it until the day of Christ Jesus.
Philippians 1:6

Z is for:

Z is for the Zest and Zeal you take on with such a Zip.

Never be lacking in zeal, but keep your spiritual fervor, serving the Lord.
Romans 12:11 NIV

*The children bring us back to God;
in eyes that dance and shine. Men read
from day to day the proof love and power divine;
for them are fathers brave and good and mothers fair and true,
for them is every cherished dream and every deed we do.*
Edgar Guest

17 Great Books for Young Children

Goodnight Moon by Margaret Wise Brown

The Velveteen Rabbit by Margery Williams

Where the Wild Things Are by Maurice Sendak

The Little Engine That Could by Watty Piper

Guess How Much I Love You by Sam McBratney

The Very Hungry Caterpillar by Eric Carle

Amelia Bedelia by Peggy Parish

Miss Rumphius by Barbara Cooney

Today I Feel Silly by Jamie Lee Curtis

The Legend of the Candy Cane by Lori Walburg

Miss Fannie's Hat by Jan Karon

Chicka Chicka ABC by Bill Martin and John Archambault

How Are You Peeling by Saxton Freymann and Joost Elffers

Jamberry by Bruce Degen

Madeline by Ludwig Bemelmans

A Pocket for Corduroy by Don Freeman

Is Your Mama a Llama? by Deborah Guarino

Home Matters

- 10 Ready, Set, Go Decorating Do's

- 9 Ways to Create an Awesome Entrance

- 10 Table Graces That Exude Style

- 5 Ways to Keep Your Home Running Smoothly

- 8 Ways to Create a Real Holiday Haven

- 12 Doughs of Christmas

- 10 Tantalizing Tree Trimmings

- 6 Alfresco-to-Go Ideas

- 6 Ideas for Mastering the Mundane

- 10 Questions to Ask When Evaluating the Comfort of Your Dining Room

- 9 Ways to Create a Signature Style for Your Home

- 5 Plate Presentations with Pizzazz

- 5 Strategies for Home Decorating

- 7 Kingdom Creations for Kids

- 7 Ways to Capture Kitchen Style

- 6 Ways to Style Up a Hallway

- 5 Patio Perk-Ups

- 9 Steps to Planning a Pretty Garden

- 7 Ideas for a Warmhearted Welcome

Home Matters

Every house where loves abides
and friendship is a guest,
Is surely home, and home, sweet home
For there the heart can rest

Henry Van Dyke

As believers in God we have three homes: our heavenly home, our family home, and our church home. In this section we will focus on our family home. As mentioned earlier, this should be a place of grace where you can relax, rejuvenate, and restore your heart and soul. Is that possible at your home? Are your living spaces inviting? Do you consider your home a haven?

A haven is a place for unwinding while finding soothing solitude and peace. Our houses, whether large or small, offer only walls and a roof. A home is created inside when we build and nurture our souls and imaginations—when our four walls adopt our personality and thus

117

become the perfect place to share ourselves. I want my home to be a welcoming environment that showers the spirit of hospitality on all who enter it.

Perhaps you desire a gathering room that is inviting, a bed and bath that works as a personal retreat, or a dining room that induces friends and family to linger after dinner. What do you think? This sounds a bit like one of those International Coffee commercials! You are probably asking if this can really be accomplished on a limited budget without a designer. Yes!

Let me tell you about our home. Is it huge? No. Did it cost a ton of money? No. Is it perfect? Heavens, no. It is a work in progress. We purchased our home from its original owners, who were in their 90s. This made for uniquely interesting décor: lamps about my height (5' 7" or so), wallpapered vanity counters, and cabinet doors looking as though they had a grill rack affixed to their fronts. Thick brown carpet throughout helped complete the "early dungeon" motif.

Fortunately we had a Realtor who, knowing we wanted hardwood floors throughout, was not afraid to pull up carpet and investigate. Overlooking areas some other people would have made a priority, we decided we liked the floor plan. When we discovered those hardwood floors under the carpet, we made our bid. Now we are living in a perpetual art project.

As always, one little idea leads to another. That next idea leads to spending more money and before you know it the garage is full of paint cans and you need new curtains.

One of my first projects was the dining room. I love dining rooms. Nothing beats good food, lots of laughter, and a comfortable place to sit and linger. Take a little peek at our dining room. Hopefully, you will see some ideas that might work in your home. Though I talk about one room only, let this room be a springboard for ideas for other sections of your home.

❤ The Dining Room

The dining room is a beautifully appointed stage on which to perform and enjoy many of life's most special events. Comfortable chairs and numerous candles create the mood for warm conversation and happy memories. Good food is great but the emphasis for a fantastic meal is more than food or beautiful surroundings. The key to wonderful dining is celebrating the chemistry of those present. It is putting those you love in the forefront, then adding the surroundings and foods as an accompaniment to enhance your time together.

Our dining room is a sunshine yellow with a honey-colored hardwood floor and pure white molding. The dark mahogany table, chairs, china cabinet, and buffet are heirlooms from my husband's family. Some of the chairs have gorgeous needlepoint covers collected by my parents at estate sales and antique auctions. (We are always looking for a few additional pieces!)

Our table seats eight, and we sometimes add similar but mismatched chairs. When the entire family arrives, we have to improvise to make everyone comfortable. Often we add a small draped table for additional seating and serve the meal by displaying our feast on the long buffet. When the meal is truly huge, I add an antique trunk at the starting point, open the lid and use the inside tray to hold plates, silverware, and napkins. It works beautifully.

I love to keep an unusual table arrangement, sometimes fresh and oftentimes silk, depicting the season. My food styling opportunities allow me to seek unique table decorations for a living. That experience makes creating the dining table for our special occasions feel like play. Mixing and matching ornate china patterns and antique glassware offer hours of enjoyment. Do not despair if your cupboard is limited. Call Grandma, Great-Aunt Lois, or even your neighbor to borrow that perfect serving piece or vase. One important way to add to the ambiance is by not limiting yourself to one pattern. Combine styles, even the elegant with the everyday, to create a whimsical and interesting tablescape.

Though the dining room is a place for celebrations, it often doubles as a work area. It all revolves around your lifestyle and the needs of your family. The off-duty dining room table, covered with pads, is a great place for collating school papers, wrapping birthday gifts, and creating flower arrangements. List the needs of your dining room, then ask, "Is it multi-functional? Does the room flow? Can I set up a beautiful buffet for impromptu guests?"

There is a well-known theory about houses. The entrance, dining and living room areas are usually formal and appear to have been covered in plastic wrap. After you pass the guest receiving areas and move into more living spaces, the middle sections of a home are less structured. By the time you reach the back, children's art is on the walls, fragrant candles are burning, and great smells are wafting from the kitchen. There is no need to separate the house to such an extreme. If you love the formal, let it be the theme throughout the home. If you are an avid fan of country chic, allow the entire home to reflect your preference. Have fun collecting and arranging pieces to make your house a home.

Whatever the condition of your home, remember a new coat of paint is the simplest face lift. Paint adds freshness and offers current colors. Sheets make great draperies and estate sales have classic items at reasonable prices. Take inventory and let your style shine. Strive to make your home a place where you and your family are aware of God's goodness while sharing His love with others.

The best houses seem to "come from the heart," and are created by people who know who they are and express it.

Charlotte Moss

10 Ready, Set, Go Decorating Do's

1. Evaluate your surroundings.

2. Devise a workable plan for creating and decorating your haven.

3. Select a style and focal point for the room.

4. Reevaluate the comfort and convenience of the room.

5. Balance the room size and furniture scale.

6. Leave open spaces so the eyes can rest.

7. Avoid making the room "untouchable" (so decorated it is not comfortable and usable).

8. Let the light shine in.

9. Add fresh touches of nature.

10. Ignore all the rules and add your own flair.

9 Ways to Create an Awesome Entrance

1. Place pots on either side of your front door and fill them with an assortment of flowers; green and white caladiums, red geraniums, and asparagus ferns make a great trio.

2. Purchase a sturdy grapevine wreath for the front door. Recycle the wreath with just a change of silk flowers. Try matching the flowers on the wreath with the flowers in the pots beside the front door.

3. If your front door has a window, drape the window with a beautiful piece of lace or a colorful silk scarf.

4. If your budget allows, purchase a gorgeous front door. Spotlight the door at night.

5. Place graduated terra-cotta pots, filled with brightly colored and fragrant flowers, on the steps leading to your front door.

6. English ivy topiaries, placed on either side of your front door, add definite grace. These should keep through each season.

7. Select a beautiful and colorful front door mat which coordinates with your flowers.

8. If your front entry is small, place one pot of flowers next to the door. This still softens your entry without taking up too much room.

9. Use an easel and chalkboard as a welcome sign. It can double as a message board, menu board, and even a spot to place a holiday greeting.

🍃 10 Table Graces That Exude Style

1. Using chargers as a frame for your china helps to coordinate the room before everyone sits down to dinner.

2. Vary your table coverings. Old sheets, quilts, and duvet covers can double as tablecloths.

3. Long, elaborate scarves or shawls make beautiful table runners.

4. Colorful napkins make perfect placemats. Place a corner of the napkin toward the center of the table and allow the opposite napkin corner to fall down the side of the table toward the chair.

5. Antique crystal salt and pepper shakers, with their tops removed, make perfect bud vases. Tie a small bow around the neck of the shaker and place one at each table setting.

6. Freshness adds style. Fill a large glass bowl with limes, lemons, oranges, or shiny red apples. Tuck taper candles amongst the fruit for use as a centerpiece.

7. For a Christmas centerpiece, fill a clear glass bowl with brightly colored Christmas balls. Tie tiny red bows to tall grapevine branches and insert the branches into the cylinder.

8. For harvesttime, fill a clear glass bowl with small fresh pumpkins, tiny green-striped gourds, and autumn leaves. Surround the bowl with English ivy.

9. Cover your table with an inexpensive white tablecloth. Using brightly colored fabric markers, write your guest's name at the top of each place setting.

10. If the theme of your evening is tropical, cover your tabletop with palm leaves or large banana leaves. Build a tropical fruit topiary in the center of the table for an edible centerpiece.

Whatever your hand finds to do, do it with all your might.
Ecclesiastes 9:10 NIV

💜 5 Ways to Keep Your Home Running Smoothly

1. Establish what "smoothly" means for you and your family. Create a clear direction for your family.

2. Have a spot for everything and try to keep everything in its spot. I am one who is pile challenged—I am working on this.

3. Plan your daily chores, projects, and cleaning so you can focus consistently.

4. Pick up the mess at night. That way each morning is a fresh new day without yesterday's clutter.

5. Your new day begins the night before. Complete as much as possible each night to ensure your new day starts smoothly (write a list of errands, prepare lunches, select clothes to wear).

The things we do at Christmas
are touched with a certain extravagance.
Robert Collier

♥ 8 Ways to Create a Real Holiday Haven

1. Purchase one petite Christmas tree for each bedroom in your home. Decorate the trees to coordinate with the style and color of each room.

2. Place a basket of seasonal goodies close to your front door. Candy canes, mini gingerbread loaves, and small jars of homemade cranberry sauce are ideas for these goodies. Give these to your guests as they leave your home.

3. A Christmas fragrance instantly provides a seasonal smile. Try evergreen and cinnamon-scented candles, holiday potpourri, and cinnamon sticks tied in bundles.

4. Save all of your children's Christmas books. Place them in baskets around the house, especially in front of the fireplace and Christmas tree.

5. Sprinkle Christmas confetti everywhere...on your tablecloth, on the packages under the tree, and inside your Christmas cards and letters.

6. Affix a fresh evergreen garland around each door frame in your home. Hang candy canes, pinecones, and ribbons on the garland.

7. Wrap your entry doors like large presents. Use six-inch ribbon down the middle and make a huge bow for the center. Spotlight the outside doors.

8. When entertaining during the Christmas season, encourage guests to mingle throughout your home. Create a roving buffet by setting up Christmas candies, bowls of punch, eggnog, and coffee in the living room, dining room, kitchen, family room, and study. Your friends and family will be able to enjoy your holiday decorations while exploring your home.

12 Doughs of Christmas

Start with a terrific sugar cookie dough, then let your imagination soar!

Ingredients:
2 cups shortening
2$\frac{1}{2}$ cups sugar
2 teaspoons vanilla
3 eggs
$\frac{1}{4}$ cup milk
6 cups flour
4$\frac{1}{2}$ teaspoons baking powder
$\frac{3}{4}$ teaspoon salt

Directions:
1. Cream shortening, sugar, and vanilla. Add eggs to creamed mixture and mix well.

2. Add milk and mix again.

3. Sift flour, baking powder, and salt. Add to creamed mixture and blend.

4. Add your favorite mix-in. (See suggestions below.)

5. Cover with plastic wrap and chill for 2 hours.

6. Bake in a 350° oven for 8–10 minutes or until golden brown.

12 Holiday Mix-Ins

1. ½ cup cranberries and ½ cup white chocolate chips

2. ½ cup chocolate chips and ½ cup crushed toffee bars

3. ½ cup red cherries and ½ cup green cherries, chopped

4. ½ cup fresh mint leaves, chopped

5. ½ cup pistachios, chopped, and ¼ cup fresh cranberries, chopped

6. 1 cup red and green M&M's

7. ½ cup candied ginger, chopped

8. 1 cup cinnamon Red Hots

9. 1 cup mint chocolate chips

10. ½ cup macadamia nuts, chopped, and ½ cup cranberries, chopped

11. ½ cup candied orange rind, chopped, and ½ cup chocolate chips

12. ⅛ cup cinnamon, ⅛ cup nutmeg, ⅛ cup powdered sugar*

* For this mix-in, roll dough out flat on a floured surface and sprinkle with swirls of cinnamon, nutmeg, and powdered sugar. Then roll dough up jelly roll fashion, slice and bake.

♥ 10 Tantalizing Tree Trimmings

1. **Beary Merry Christmas**—Gather stuffed bears of all sizes and colors. Select a ribbon color that will coordinate with your gift wrap and use it to tie big ribbons around each bear's neck. On the back of the ribbon stick a little ornament hanger and hang the bow-tied bears all over the tree.

2. **Pinecones and Holly Berries**—Collect pinecones throughout the year. As the Yuletide season approaches, begin tying plaid ribbons to the top stem of each pinecone. Purchase artificial holly berry stems. Remove the stem and string the greenery and berries onto a heavy string. Starting at the top of the Christmas tree, wrap the holly berry garland all the way down to the bottom of the tree. Fill in the spaces with the plaid-ribboned pinecones.

3. **Candy Cane Lane**—Basic dough recipe: 2 cups flour, 1 cup salt, 1 cup cold water, and 1 teaspoon peppermint extract. Stir together. Knead the mixture until it forms a stiff dough. To add colors, take small portions of the dough and work in little dabs of paste food coloring until you reach your red shade for the candy canes. Color the white portion with washable white acrylic paint. Roll equal-sized pieces of each color into ropes and twist them together. Cut the twisted strip to the desired lengths and bend the top to form a curved top. Dry candy canes in a 325° oven for one to two hours. Dip in paraffin to coat. Tie a huge red and white striped bow and top the tree. Leave long streamers coming from the bow to tuck and twist throughout the tree. Tie the various candy cane sizes onto the tree with bright green ribbons.

4. **Twelve Days of Christmas**—Make small copies of the musical score to "The Twelve Days of Christmas." Start decorating the tree with the classic song. Fill in the empty areas with partridges, pear trees, little drums, gold rings, two turtle doves, four calling birds, and a few French hens.

5. **We Three Kings**—Crowns, jewels, and more. Frame the bottom of this tree with a large purple robe, one fit for a king. Decorate the tree with mini crowns (found at most craft stores). Make a garland of star shapes and shiny beads to represent the star the Wise Men followed in search of baby Jesus.

6. **Helping-Hand Mittens**—This tree is a burst of color. Make salt-dough hand ornaments by using a hand-shaped cookie cutter. Purchase several pairs of colorful mittens. After making the hand ornaments, paint the nails and accessorize with shiny bead jewel "rings." Tie the decorated hand ornaments to the tree with coordinating ribbons. Place the colorful mittens in between the hands for extra color.

7. **Stocking Tree**—Stockings old and new, borrowed and blue make this tree a step above. Collect stockings from tag sales, Christmas stores, and old attics. Purchase some gold cording and tie the stockings to the tree.

8. **Treasure Tree**—Little treasure chests and petite boxes wrapped in Christmas paper are the "stars" of this tree. Hot glue ornament hangers to the little treasure chests (available at most craft stores.) Thread sparkling beads onto a gold cord and wrap the glittery cord around the tree.

9. **Hearts and Tarts**—Heart-shaped cookie cutters take center stage here. Big red and green ribbons tie the heart shapes to the tree. Prepare fragrant holiday ornaments (see #3, Candy Cane Lane, for recipe) in heart shapes, make a hole at top of heart with a straw, and thread onto a long holiday patterned ribbon. Wrap the ornament garland around the tree.

10. **Adoring Angel**—This is an angel collector's dream tree. Angels of all shapes and sizes grace the branches

of this Christmas tree. Wrap star garland all around the tree and then fill in the spaces with angels. Tuck in several shiny halos and sprinkle with angel dust for a heavenly touch.

Oh, how good everything tasted in that bower, with the fresh wind rustling the poplar leaves, sunshine and sweet wood-smells about them, and birds singing overhead.

Susan Coolidge

❤ 6 Alfresco-to-Go Ideas

1. Fill your car or van with plenty of warm blankets, great food, and lots of good friends. Open the windows, play Christmas carols, and wish all a "Merry Christmas!" Try a tailgate party with mugs of cinnamon hot cocoa and Christmas cookies.

2. College weekend tailgates are great. Ambiance on the asphalt begins with picnic baskets, wooden crates, or decorative boxes to pack the following: paper plates, cups, bowls, eating and serving utensils, a cutting board, napkins, paper towels, wet wipes, plastic drop cloth, tablecloth, bottle opener, garbage bags, emergency first-aid kit, large Ziploc bags filled with insect repellent, small packages of condiments, folding

chairs, and, of course, food. Music and games provide further fun.

3. Pack your picnic by the lake in wooden crates, found in the back of most grocery stores. Ask your kids to splatter paint the crates. After they dry, pack your feast in the cute crates. Turn these crates over at the picnic site, and they double as little individual tables and chairs.

4. Pack the pillows. If you don't want decorative pillows ruined, place them in a colorful pillowcase and tie the ends off with a ribbon.

5. Fill galvanized buckets with fresh daisies. Use this as a centerpiece to turn a roadside picnic table from ordinary to casual chic. If you're on your way to visit friends, your picnic centerpiece will make a perfect hostess gift.

6. Place two old sheets on your den floor, pile on your picnic supplies, fold the sides of the sheets over the contents, and tie in a big knot. This big knapsack will help reduce your trips to the car when you reach your destination.

The true calling of a Christian is not to do extraordinary things, but to do ordinary things in an extraordinary way.

Dean Stanley

♥ 6 Ideas for Mastering the Mundane

1. Complete the jobs you dislike first, then you do not have to dread them the whole day.

2. Make sorting laundry a game your kids can play. Purchase laundry bags, white one for the whites, colored one for the colors, purple one for the towels, etc. Hang these in your laundry room or on hooks in the bathroom and the laundry has sorted itself (theoretically).

3. Make rotating grocery lists—a big list for when everything needs to be replenished and a reduced list for when the staples are not needed.

4. Plan menus for two weeks at a time. Include several quick fixes or pantry picks so that dinner can be done on the double. Rotate and mix and match those menus, and your month of menus is ready.

5. Simplicity helps us keep order. Keep things simple.

6. When the mundane overwhelms you, shift into a lower gear. Play classical music when you need to relax and take some personal moments to refocus your thoughts when the mundane looms large.

♥ 10 Questions to Ask When Evaluating the Comfort of Your Dining Room.

1. Start with the frame of the room, the walls. Are they the color you like?

2. Do the window treatments convey a style you love?

3. Is the furniture functional?

4. Do you have the space you need?

5. Can you seat guests comfortably?

6. Do you have a plan for a very large group?

7. Is everything accessible?

8. Can you bring food in and out successfully?

9. Do you have good storage for linens, china, and stemware?

10. Is the dining spot a comfortable, inviting place to linger, and a suitable spot for marathon holiday meals?

Duty makes us do things well,
but love makes us do them beautifully.

Phillip Brooks

❤ 9 Ways to Create a Signature Style for Your Home

1. Your entryway can set the mood of your home. Create this area so that it reflects the things you love. Save and

frame greeting cards, fill beautiful vases with fresh or silk flowers, set out fragrant potpourri.

2. Select a color theme. Vary the theme by varying the shades of your chosen colors throughout your home.

3. Don't limit yourself to just putting pictures in frames. Frame baby dedication clothes, army medals, hats, gloves, antique glasses, mirrors, preschool artwork, unique cards, watches, sports equipment, and so on.

4. Stencil your favorite pattern in different shapes and sizes throughout the house. If you like hearts, stencil the ceiling in your child's room with different colored hearts and bring a similar design down the hallway in another color family.

5. On your mantel, vary vase heights, candlesticks, picture frames, or a favorite collection of clocks or old books.

6. Choose accents with impact. Select a fire-engine-red lamp to liven up a dusty blue room. Repeat that same process from room to room. Add color splashes with pillows, blankets, foot stools, and picture frames.

7. Turn antique dresser mirrors into picture frames. When hunting antiques you often find the dresser mirror frames without the mirror. Use the old wooden shape for matting and framing a large picture. This also works with window frames.

8. Change all the knobs in your home to match the style and flair of your different rooms—flower-shaped knobs work great in a girl's room, truck-shaped knobs work great in a boy's room.

9. Save old silk scarves and blouses for recovering lampshades. Pretty silk flowers, tied bows, and buttons also make a lamp shade interesting.

5 Plate Presentations with Pizzazz

1. Using a damp pastry brush or a damp paper towel, rub the outside perimeter of your dinner plate. Sprinkle the damp surface with freshly chopped herbs.

2. Stencil your dessert plates. Place a simple stencil on the side of your dessert plate and dust with cocoa powder.

3. Paint a fresh rose with beaten egg white. Dip the egg-painted rose in sugar for a fresh glisten to the top of a cake.

4. Mashed potato towers make your plate look unique. Make a tower in the center of your dinner plate and surround your tower with meat slices and vegetables. Place a fresh herb sprig on the top.

5. Finely shred several colors of cabbage. Place a layer of the cabbage over the entire surface of your dinner plate. Pull the leaves off of a purple cabbage and use those as individual serving bowls for your menu items.

What Does the Bible Say About Hospitality?

Be devoted to one another in brotherly love; give preference to one another in honor; not lagging behind in diligence, fervent in spirit, serving the Lord; rejoicing in hope, persevering in tribulation, devoted to prayer, contributing to the needs of the saints, practicing hospitality.
Romans 12:10-13

Do not neglect to show hospitality to strangers, for by this some have entertained angels without knowing it.
Hebrews 13:2

Be hospitable to one another without complaint.
1 Peter 4:9

This is really the jolliest little place I ever was in. Now, wherever did you pick up those prints? Make the place look so home-like, they do. No wonder you're so fond of it, Mole. Tell us all about it, and how you came to make it what it is.

Kenneth Grahame, *The Wind in the Willows*

💜 5 Strategies for Home Decorating

1. What is your style? Where do you feel most comfortable? Is it that overstuffed chair that you sink into as if you will never have to get out? Is it a chaise lounge covered in chintz? Is it a taupe-colored leather sofa with no pillows? Take an afternoon, go to several furniture stores from upscale to resale and find what makes you comfortable. On this trip don't look at price tags. Look at what you love.

2. Before returning home from your shopping tour, drop by a great bookstore that offers a wide variety of home magazines—I love *Martha Stewart Living, Elle Decor, Southern Living, Victoria,* and *Veranda.* Look through the magazines and tear out the pictures that best suit your decorating taste. File these according to room, color schemes, themes, and accessory ideas.

3. Visit paint stores—Home Depot, Lowes, and other large home remodeling centers have extensive paint departments. Look for your favorite colors, techniques, and finishes for selecting a room's background hue. They have lots of the little sample paint chips you can bring home. Get ones in the same color family, but in different hues so if one is too light or dark you can have a point of comparison.

4. Sit and think. What houses have you visited that you loved? Was it the wall color, the furniture, the carpet or hardwood floors, the rugs, plants, or wall art? Think about this. Why did you like it? What feeling from

those homes you like do you want to duplicate in your own home?

5. In *Chris Madden's Guide to Personalizing Your Home,* Chris offers five style preferences: traditional (classic and history minded), contemporary (clean, sleek, and modern), adventurous (eclectic, lots of color and texture), romantic (surrounded in family pieces and soft fabrics), serene (less is more, creamy taupe and neutrals). Do you see one here that fits your taste?

💜 7 Kingdom Creations for Kids

1. If your children are old enough, allow them to choose their room's color palette. If the thought of that stresses you, preselect several options you can live with and let them have the final choice.

2. Cut a two-inch-thick dowel rod the length of your floor to ceiling. Screw numerous cup hooks into the rod from the top to the bottom. Position the rod in a corner of the room (this should be taut and secure between the ceiling and the floor). Hang stuffed animals, dolls, and toys on the hooks. This is a great storage method and looks cute in the corner of your child's room.

3. Kitty Bartholomew, interior designer, made these suggestions for adding style to old furniture: "A fresh coat of crisp white paint adds life to furniture. To make an old piece more unique, affix laminated maps to the

headboard and footboard of a bed. Using a hot glue gun, outline the bed with sisal rope."

4. Old and empty frames make perfect painting projects. Spray paint frames white and then stencil or paint to match the theme of your child's room. Try polka dots, small heart stencils, little plastic airplanes glued to the perimeter of the frame, silk flowers, and so on. Once the frame is made, coordinate the print to make interesting wall art.

5. Try hammering wooden crates at the top of the wall directly under the ceiling on one side of the room. This makes an interesting display case for trains, Barbies, stuffed animals, sports trophies, and other wonderful things your kids collect.

6. Select a theme and decorate the room around this theme using colors and objects you love. For example, stencil trucks on one wall, purchase a throw rug with a road and truck motif, turn a big dump truck into the base of a lamp, and make truck-shaped pillows for the bed.

7. Frame and hang your children's favorite art creations. Place these in their room or down your hallway as your family's personal "art gallery."

I know I'm home by the fragrance of my mother's kitchen.

Susan Wales

♥ 7 Ways to Capture Kitchen Style

1. Make a garland with cookie cutters. Tie the cutters with colorful ribbon or raffia and drape around a window, over a door, or down a wall.

2. Stencil a fruit pattern down one wall. Match the fabric on your seat covers with a fruit-print fabric.

3. The kitchen is often the gathering place in a home. Look at your kitchen and see if there are some nooks that need some spice. Try hanging herb plants, placing a ceramic pitcher filled with wooden cooking utensils, adding a bright table runner, or setting individual pots of herbs or flowers on your windowsill.

4. Keep countertops clear, leaving room for a beautiful bowl of fresh fruit or a collection of interesting canisters.

5. When entertaining casually, a graduated three-tiered metal hanging basket works beautifully for freeing room on your buffet. Use the top basket for eating utensils, the middle basket for napkins and the bottom basket for fresh bread. Put a small plant hook in your ceiling and tie the basket to the hook with a ribbon.

6. Purchase a distressed table at an estate sale or flea market. Create a colorful design on the tabletop with interesting tiles. Many home improvement stores offer classes on decorative tiling.

7. Pour your dishwashing soap into a beautiful tall glass bottle. Select a color that adds brightness to your room.

💜 6 Ways to Style Up a Hallway

1. Select a theme for your hallway. Some ideas are family pictures (for example, all in black and white with red mattes), pet pictures, favorite scenery from your most cherished trips, or a year-by-year picture diary of your children. Uniquely framed and matted photos instantly add style to a hallway.

2. Create an indoor garden mural down your hallway. Nail wooden pickets to the wall and stencil ivy and colorful flowers in between the pickets and up above the pickets.

3. Put a chair rail down the middle of each wall on either side of the hallway. Paint under the chair rail with one of your favorite colors.

4. Use the hallway for the children's art gallery. Frame their favorite selections from a year of school art projects and hang them in the hall gallery.

5. Line the hallway with unique baskets. Place plants in some, magazines in others. Leave some empty just in case you need a quick way to deliver a gift.

6. This is a great place to display antique quilts. Affix quilts to the wall with special hangers or quilt racks so as not to ruin the quilt.

*Color is like food for the spirit—plus it's
not addictive or fattening.*

Isaac Mizrahi

♥ 5 Patio Perk-Ups

1. Purchase an inexpensive baker's rack, and fill it full of colorful plants and pottery. Intersperse a few citronella candles to keep the bugs at bay.

2. A wooden slatted swing or glider is a wonderful way to relax. Place one on the patio to add a serene and relaxed touch. Fill it with fluffy pillows.

3. Use brightly colored pillow cushions on your patio chairs.

4. Tender-sounding wind chimes make a lovely addition and a soft and beautiful sound on breezy days.

5. Purchase a colorful door mat that coordinates with your flower selections.

♥ 9 Steps to Planning a Pretty Garden

1. Plan your garden first. Is it the front yard you want to redo or spruce up? Is it that bare backyard? Is it both?

2. Read up on your region. The house and garden section of your newspaper is a great source of information, as well as magazines and the Internet. One mistake I made was wanting low-sun plants in the front yard, where full sun existed most of the day. Knowledge of your region and your yard saves time, money, and extra hard work.

3. Choose plant items that are easy to care for. Often the expensive nursery has a great horticulturist on hand that can answer questions. You can buy a few plants there and then fill in from a cheaper source.

4. Keep in mind your budget and time restraints. You can spend a bundle rather fast. Make your plan and work it.

5. Try container gardening. This is a good way to add color in various areas, and you can always rearrange if you need color somewhere else. Try plants like snapdragons, zinnias, sunflowers, and impatiens, to name a few.

6. Make sure you have the correct gardening tools. A good spade, shovel, rake, leaf rake, and hoe make the job simpler.

7. Do not forget to protect yourself as you beautify your yard. You will need gardening gloves, sunscreen, a lightweight hat, and lightweight clothes.

8. Water, feed, and watch for bugs. When unusual things begin happening with my plants, I always pinch off a leaf and head to the plant doctor. They can usually look at a plant and decide what it needs to become healthy again.

9. Everything looks better when a few weeds are pulled. It feels like a good haircut!

7 Ideas for a Warmhearted Welcome from Welcome Home by Emilie Barnes

1. What aspect of your home or apartment do you enjoy most: the view, the quiet, the yard? Let that aspect be the focus of your hospitality. Share the aspects of your life that bring you the most pleasure.

2. Have fun giving guests and family members the royal treatment. Make a crown out of gold paper and take it to your guest room along with breakfast in bed or use it to designate a guest of honor at a meal.

3. Piles of pillows are a relatively inexpensive way to add a luxuriously hospitable touch to any room. Big European pillows are nice for reading in bed.

4. One of the big hits in our guest bathroom is a big, fluffy terry robe hanging on the back of the bathroom door. If you love that in fancy hotels, why not invest in your own at home?

5. Save the complimentary bottles of shampoo and lotion, the little sewing kits, and shoeshine cloths you receive in nice hotels, or buy them from the travel-size area in your drugstore. Include a toothbrush and toothpaste. Place in a pretty basket in your guest's bathroom.

6. Basics can make a big difference to the experience of hospitality. Is there plenty of toilet paper in the bathroom your guests use? Are there extra towels?

7. Try putting an overnight guest in your child's room for the night and give your child the "privilege" of camping out in the living room. The result: an adventure for your child and welcome privacy for your guest.

Family and Friends Matter

- 7 Ways to Weave God into Your Family's Day

- 6 Ideas for Building a Firm Family Foundation

- 6 Ways to a Smooth Sunday Morning

- 8 "Themed" Potluck Buffet Menu Ideas That Make a Great Party

- 10 Ideas for Creating Dinner on the Double

- 6 Ways to Reach Out to Your Neighbors

- 10 Ways to Simplify Sharing

- 6 Ways to Shop and Share

- 6 Easy Friendship Baskets

- 5 Signature Wraps That Say "I Love You"

- 6 Hospitality Helpers

- 5 Easy, Elegant, and Extravagant Easter Ideas

- 5 Family Traditions That Last a Lifetime

- 14 Steps to an Organized Household

- 6 Strategies for Having More Family Time

- 4 Ideas for Thanksgiving Treats

- 25 Homemade and Heartfelt Christmas Traditions

- 3 Ways to Be a Good Mom and a Good Friend Too

Family and Friends Matter

*The best relationships...are built up like a fine lacquer finish,
with accumulated layers made of many little acts of love.*

Gilbert and Bradshaw

After God, family and friends are two important foundational stones in our lives. The family teaches us basic values, life skills, and, hopefully, how to live a responsible and Christ-centered life. Unhappily, not everyone experiences that type of upbringing. Either way, our lives are greatly influenced by mom and dad, grandmom and granddad, and aunts and uncles. Our friends also play a big part in our lives. They are the ones who share our joys as well as our sorrows. None of us have the idyllic life depicted in 1950s sitcoms. We face tragedy, misfortune, illness, and numerous other opportunities to grow in character and strength. Our selection of the people with whom we share life makes a difference. Teaching our children to select friends wisely is a gift we give them. The security of knowing they are with people who share their values and beliefs is a reassurance for us.

As I was growing up, our family had several rituals. One was a large Saturday morning brunch. We slept late, and then prepared a cholesterol feast: fried eggs, cheese rice, biscuits, and fried potatoes and onions with some sort of fruit. As I write these words, I can smell the aroma of a house full of love and the essence of good grease. To this day I love breakfast.

Another of our rituals was a big Thanksgiving weekend extravaganza. My mom's father was a grocer, and our family events always focused on the table. (Are my reasons for entering the food business becoming clearer?) We prepared recipes from Grandmother's cookbook and tasted creations in various stages as they were being prepared for the meal. Marshmallow salad, cornbread dressing, and a turkey that baked all night were just part of the banquet table. With stomachs still full, we always had a BIG day of shopping

Not all of our traditions centered on kitchen preparation. We also had our own pew at the First Baptist Church in Marion, Illinois. Yes, that is right. Our names weren't on the pew, but it was our tradition to be third row back, center section. In the smaller Baptist churches, everyone seemed to have their spot. My brother and I did not sit with the youth group unless we were singing with the choir; we sat with our parents in OUR pew. I liked that. It was where we worshiped together as a family, and where our friends knew we would be.

Friends are so important. A friend is one you can talk to, one who understands your world, difficulties, and triumphs. Thinking of my favorite friends always makes me smile because of all the shared laughter, tears, prayers, and love. Often our get-togethers revolve around food. We meet at restaurants, we meet at each other's homes for dinner, or we meet at an amusement park to enjoy the day. Life would lose its richness without the opportunity to live it with friends.

Honestly, most of my friends have over-the-top senses of humor. We spend a good portion of our time laughing at something, whether it's a college prank or a funny semi-disaster at a child's birthday party. Friends that enjoy a long history have their own special rituals and traditions, and the happiness of hours with close friends cannot be described. Along with the love and support of family, friends offer joy, share the burdens, and lighten the load. They are priceless.

This section will give you some solid ideas for nurturing and building relationships with family and friends that pray, play, and stay together. Think of it as little bricks to lay on a pathway to eternity.

If you discern God's love in every moment of happiness,
you will multiply a thousandfold your capacity
to fully enjoy your blessings.

Frances J. Roberts

♥ 7 Ways to Weave God into Your Family's Day

1. Live your life with a strong eternal perspective, showing your children a genuine faith, not a Sunday morning faith.

2. Remove anything in your life that would keep you from God's best. Ask your children, "Is that decision God's best for your life?"

3. Pray spontaneously. Make it a natural part of your day, not a pious ritual. As Cheri Fuller explains in her book *When Families Pray*, "If you want your children to learn to pray on the spot, model that kind of prayer. When your children approach you with a worry or a problem, pray about it with them. Praying spontaneous prayers like these shows your children that God cares about every part of their lives."

4. Choose to serve God as a family.

5. Cleanse your heart of covetousness by being content with what you have.

6. Pursue a close relationship with God. Spend time resting in His presence.

7. My friend and neighbor, Mary Sheppard, is a busy mother of four; however, each day she leaves Bible verses on her children's desks for them to look up and read. This is a great way to emphasize Scripture reading to your children.

♥ 6 Ideas for Building a Firm Family Foundation

1. Leave notes in unexpected spots. For example, in the footy part of a child's pj's, on a pillow, in a lunch box, on a bathroom mirror, etc.

2. Look into your loved one's eyes, smile, and listen.

3. Give big hugs often. I strive for a minimum of eight a day.

4. Have humor breaks that involve everyone.

5. Take time to talk.

6. Share hospitality with other families.

♥ 6 Ways to a Smooth Sunday Morning

1. Start the night before. Select clothes, iron clothes, find the lost shoe, and put your Bibles and notebooks in the car.

2. Chart out the morning's chain of events, especially for the little ones. That way they will know what is expected of them, and they can choose to be team players.

3. Play beautiful and relaxing praise music while everyone is getting ready for church.

4. Pray that your morning will be a smooth one.

5. Set your alarm a bit earlier so you can have your face washed and makeup started.

6. Plan a very quick but nourishing breakfast.

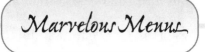

Marvelous Menus

💜 8 "Themed" Potluck Buffet Menu Ideas That Make a Great Party

These are party and menu ideas just to get you started. Pull out your favorite cookbooks and use these ideas as a springboard for creating your own signature style party.

1. Soup Pa De Do Da

Chicken and sausage cassoulet
Savory cheesecake with homemade croutons
Rustic breads with chive butter
Pumpkin bread pudding with cinnamon cream

Food for the Little Eaters:
Chicken pops
Bread batons with butter
Carrot curls and dip
Pumpkin bread slices

2. An Evening of Elegance

Mustard honey roasted pork tenderloin

Garlic cheese polenta
Green bean and red pepper bundles
Sun-dried tomato muffins
Chocolate mousse tart

Food for the Little Eaters:
Pork pockets
Polenta shapes
Cheese muffins
Oversized chocolate chip cookies

3. Brunch for a Bunch

Omelet casserole
Apricot and pear turnovers
Ginger scones with smoked turkey and sweet mustard
Cheese board
Baked fruits
Ice cream parfaits

Food for the Little Eaters:
Little piggy biscuits
Turnovers
Turkey scramble
Cheese
Fruits
Ice cream sprinkle sundaes

4. Garden Party

Chilled peach soup with raspberry swirls
Grilled chicken and three-pepper kabobs
Cold pesto pasta salad

Three-green salad with citrus vinaigrette
Flowerpot breads
Meringues with ice cream and chocolates

Food for the Little Eaters:
Kid kabobs
Alphabet pasta and cheese
Flowerpot breads
Ice cream sundaes

5. Sunday Lunch After Church

Chicken and vegetable rolls
Garlic mashed potato soufflé
Papaya coleslaw
Sour cream biscuits
Kiwi pie

Food for the Little Eaters:
Chicken chunks
Smashed potatoes
Lettuce dippers
Sour cream biscuits
Fruit cup with marshmallow topping

6. A Relaxed Saturday Night

Turkey burger buffet
Condiment tray (bacon, lettuces, relishes, grilled onions, cheeses, mustards)
Assorted buns
Sweet potato fries
Garlic molasses baked beans
5-topping brownies

Food for the Little Eaters:
Popcorn pouches
Mini bagel burgers
Sweet potato fries
Fresh vegetable mix
Five-topping brownies

7. Thrill'n and Grill'n

Grilled red pepper and corn chowder
Grilled chicken and wild rice packets
Roasted vegetables
Potato, onion, and fresh herbs
Grilled garlic French bread
Grilled pound cake with fruit sauce and vanilla cream

Food for the Little Eaters:
Corn chowder
Grilled chicken on a stick
Savory potato wedges
Pound cake alphabet with dipping sauces

8. Back Porch Pick-ups

Beef and lettuce roll-ups
Savory cheese straws
Spud slices with bacon and chives
Ham triangles
Fresh strawberries with chocolate powdered sugar
Tropical cheesecake bites

Food for the Little Eaters:
Sandwich shapes

Cheese straws
Spud buddies
Ham triangles
Strawberries
Fruit ices

Spice a dish with love, and it pleases every palate.

Plautus

♥ 10 Ideas for Creating Dinner on the Double

1. Have a planned and prepared pantry—you probably have a meal just waiting to happen. Helpful and versatile items are things like garlic, onions, potatoes, pasta, canned white chicken, brown rice, quick cooking polenta, and stewed tomatoes.

2. The tortilla is your friend! Paint several (eight-inch) flour tortillas with melted butter and push the middle of each tortilla into a large muffin tin (sides will stick up, should resemble a bowl shape). Place in a 350° oven and bake until toasted, about 10 to 12 minutes. While the tortillas are baking, scramble some eggs, add some cooked and crumbled bacon, and spoon into the tortilla bowl. Serve with a fresh fruit salad.

3. Prepare fettuccini according to package directions, drain and toss with a drained can of albacore tuna, canned artichoke hearts, and stewed tomatoes. Serve with breadsticks and crisp salad from a bag.

4. Pound thawed chicken breast between two sheets of waxed paper. Place 2 tablespoons oil and 1 tablespoon balsamic vinegar into a skillet, sauté the chicken breast turning once. Add a can of stewed tomatoes and a teaspoon of balsamic vinegar, cover and simmer for 10 minutes. Serve over quick-cooked brown rice.

5. Drop by your favorite salad bar and select the freshest and prettiest vegetables. Place the vegetables in a resealable plastic bag, add fresh chopped garlic, 2 tablespoons olive oil, fresh chopped herbs of choice, seal the bag and shake to coat the vegetables. Place on a cookie sheet and broil until browned, stirring once or twice during cooking. Serve over pasta, rice, or polenta.

6. Keep copies of tried-and-true fast recipes at your fingertips for instant reference.

7. Be sure and read through the entire recipe before you start, then set out all the ingredients you will need.

8. Keep cooked rice (add a little water to reheat), pasta, bread, rolls, biscuits, and muffins in the freezer ready to thaw and heat when needed.

9. Set the table the night before or after breakfast. Better yet, let your kids set the table.

10. Periodically make enough food for two meals and freeze one batch. Good two-for-oners are soups, stews, chili, pasta sauce, meatballs, and casseroles.

Tips for Keeping Mealtime Special

1. Turn off the television and ignore the telephone.

2. Stimulate good conversation by asking a question at the table that each person must answer. Ask questions for which there is no right or wrong answer, and everyone will have an answer. Some examples are, "What is the scariest storm you've ever lived through?" or "What is one thing you did today that you feel good about?"

3. Involve family members in the meal preparation and cleanup.

4. Eat at a set table for your family meal and encourage good manners.

5. Cultivate a relaxed attitude about having company. Everyone appreciates a warm meal and good conversation. It does not have to be fancy.

From *Table Talk* by Mimi Wilson and Mary Beth Lagerborg.

Share your life, and find the finest joy man can know. Do not be stingy with your heart. Get out of yourself into the lives of others, and new life will flow into you—share and share alike.

Joseph Fort Newton

6 Ways to Reach Out to Your Neighbors

1. Borrow some sugar and return it two-fold. Bring back a little bag of sugar and a batch of fresh-baked cookies or brownies.

2. Take an interest in their lives and the lives of their children.

3. Help coordinate an annual neighborhood "dinner on the grounds." Ask the neighbor who has the biggest trees to host the outdoor event so there will be plenty of shade.

4. Invite your neighbors over for coffee and a snack. This simple gesture will give you an opportunity to get to know each other.

5. Have on hand a supply of ice cream, cookies, and lemonade, and invite the neighborhood children over to play.

6. Bake extra goodies during the holidays, place in Chinese take-out containers decorated with a bow, and deliver these to your neighbors.

♥ 10 Ways to Simplify Sharing

1. Create a plan to work sharing into your lifestyle. Make a sharing calendar, a month-by-month idea planner for reaching out to others.

2. Select a person or family that needs to see love in action. Show them love by sharing your food, books, clothes, and, most importantly, your time.

3. When preparing a meal, double up your ingredients. Make two or three batches and freeze for an emergency hospitality call.

4. Stock a gift closet for children and adults. This prevents being caught without a gift and saves money when your favorite items go on sale.

5. Purchase numerous cards that fit every occasion. Mark your calendar, grab a card, and mail it.

6. A "thinking of you" phone call can be a special pick-me-up to someone feeling down.

7. Pray for a friend regularly. Ask them how to pray for them specifically.

8. Purchase several inspirational books that are easy to mail. Mark a passage that has helped you through a difficult time, write a note to slip inside, and drop in the mail.

9. Do something nice for the children of a friend.

10. Bottom line for sharing with simplicity: open door, stocked refrigerator, listening ears.

6 Ways to Shop and Share

In Ellie Kay's bestselling book *Shop, Save and Share*, she explains, "When you shop to share you become God's provision for others." Here she shares six ways to accomplish your savings so sharing is a cinch:

1. Clip coupons and highlight the expiration date. You can send expired coupons to military families stationed overseas. They are good up to six months past the expiration date in overseas commissaries.

2. Organize your coupons alphabetically, using the most prominent name on the coupon.

3. Take advantage of savings combinations by using a store's coupon in conjunction with a manufacturer's coupon.

4. Take your list and do not leave home without it.

5. Using an aisle order chart, make your lists by aisle. This is a real time-saver.

6. Double your savings. Shop at stores that offer double coupons.

The smallest acts of kindness are worth more than the grandest intention.
Author Unknown

Party Planners

❤ 6 Easy Friendship Baskets

1. **Bar-be-que Basket**—Line a basket with a red-and-white checked tablecloth, fill with plastic corn on the cob containers, a petite citron candle, flashy red-and-white napkins, a long-handled bar-be-que brush, your favorite gourmet sauces, your best picnic recipe, bug repellent, and colored plastic cups and plates.

2. **Beach Basket**—Line a basket with a soft floral beach towel. Fill the basket with suntan oil, a beach ball, a shovel and pail, moist hand wipes, flip-flop shoes, and a Beach Boys tape.

3. **Relaxation Basket**—Line a basket with a soft floral bath towel. Fill the basket with fragrant votive candles (try getting the same fragrance as the flowers on your bath towel), add a container of bath salts, bath oils, moisturizers, and a CD or tape of classical music.

4. **Garden Variety Basket**—Line a basket with small plastic bags. Fill the basket with small gardening hand tools, bug repellent, floral gardening gloves, a great straw hat, suntan lotion, bulbs, and a six-pack of your friend's favorite bedding plants.

5. **Afternoon of Fun Basket**—Line a basket with the comic section of the newspaper. Fill the basket with silly putty, face paints, a jar full of stringable beads,

plastic strings to string the beads on, a great funny movie, microwave popcorn, M&M's, washable paints and sponges, solid-color paint smocks, and crazy straws.

6. **Favorites basket**—Line a basket with your favorite color of tissue paper. Fill the basket with your favorite things: favorite candy, favorite fruit, a gift certificate to your favorite music store, your favorite book, and a gift certificate to your favorite ice cream store.

♥ 5 Signature Wraps That Say "I Love You"

1. **Hearts and Stars**—A roll of white butcher paper is a perfect addition to your wrapping paper stash. A couple of heart-shaped and star-shaped sponges and colorful paints can transform plain white paper into an individually unique work of art. Roll out the paper and stamp away. Next to the hearts write, "You are loved." Next to the stars write, "You are a shining star."

2. **Colored Netting**—Fabric stores have great wrapping paper alternatives! Buy netting to accommodate the size of the gift. Place the gift inside and pull the netting up over the gift. Secure with a rubber band. Roll another section of netting into a long tube shape and make a large bow to cover the rubber band.

3. **Aluminum Foil**—Pull out several long sheets of foil, place your gift in the center, pull the foil up and around the gift, and twist like a Hershey's KISS. Tuck a

note in the top on some white paper so it resembles the top of a chocolate kiss. A great gift wrap for a chocolate lover!

4. **Glass Carafes**—Fill a glass carafe halfway with little pebbles, small shells, pennies, or corn kernels. Place a small gift in the middle and fill the rest with the same items or combination of items until the gift is covered. Place a small handkerchief on the top of the carafe and secure it with a rubber band and a colorful ribbon. This will be like finding a prize in a Cracker Jack box.

5. **Mailing Tubes**—You can find mailing tubes in all different colors. Select your favorite and decorate with stamps, stickers, and small ribbons. Fill the inside of the tube with confetti, dried beans, small pine cones, shredded paper, or fabric. Place your gift inside and seal it with a lid. (You may want to issue a word of warning before the confetti flies everywhere.)

6 Hospitality Helpers

Prior to the nuts and bolts of party planning, here are six simple suggestions that are foundational to hospitality:

1. Provide a relaxed and peaceful atmosphere. You are the thermostat of the event. Plan ahead so you can be relaxed and peaceful.

2. Offer a gracious greeting. Be at the door when they arrive.

3. Decide on a simple schedule of events. Have a written agenda as to what will happen when and use it as your guide.

4. Serve your guests comfortably. If you are not a formal person, do not use china. Serve to your comfort level.

5. Plan for great table conversation. Have a conversation plan and speak with your husband about the new happenings in the lives of your guests. Think of common topics if other guests do not know each other.

6. Extend gracious goodbyes. Walk your guests to the car. Have ready a simple gift, such as a small loaf of bread, or small box of candy.

My home is a treasure chest, in which
I collect memories of my family and friends.
Clara Ferree Smith

❤ 5 Easy, Elegant, and Extravagant Easter Ideas

Easter is a joyous time when we remember that Jesus Christ came back to life after paying the penalty for our sin. It is a holy holiday celebrating the fact that by accepting His death on the cross, and believing in His resurrection, we might live with Him in eternity and personally know His love in the present.

1. Try making an Easter tree as the focal point of your Easter decorating.

The Easter Tree

Things you will need:

basic dough recipe (2 cups flour, 1 cup salt, 1 cup cold water)

rolling pin

cookie cutters or patterns (cross, dove, angels, and lily)

straw

plastic wrap

ribbon

sturdy branch

large piece of Styrofoam

Easter grass

large container

Instructions:

- Prepare dough by sifting together flour, salt, and water. Knead the mixture until it forms a medium-stiff, smooth dough. If needed, add more flour to stiffen the dough.

- To add color, take a small portion of the dough and work in little dabs of paste food coloring until you get the shade you want. For white dough, mix in washable acrylic paint. Store any unused dough in plastic bags in the refrigerator until you are ready to make your Easter ornaments.

- Place a small amount of flour on a waxed paper-covered surface. Use a rolling pin to roll out the dough to a ½-inch thickness. Dip the cookie cutter in flour and cut out the shapes. (If you cannot find the Christian Easter symbols as cookie cutters, make a master pattern from cardboard and cut around the shape with a kitchen knife.)

- Once each symbol is cut, insert a straw about ½-inch down from the top of the shape. This makes a hole so the ornaments can be hung on the tree.

- Place on a cookie sheet. Dry the ornaments in a 325° oven for 1 to 2 hours or until the ornaments feel hard to the touch.

Tree preparation:

Place the large piece of Styrofoam into the container. Insert the branch into the Styrofoam. Cover the Styrofoam with Easter grass.

2. Dye interesting eggs and place them in a crystal bowl to add color to your dining room, entry, or Easter baskets.

Rubber-band-Dyed Eggs

Things you will need:

eggs
saucepan
water
newspapers
rubber bands of different widths
egg dye
bowl
large spoon
paper towels

Instructions:

- ❤ Boil the eggs for 13 minutes.

- ❤ Run the eggs under cold water until they are cool.

- ❤ Spread newspapers on your worktable.

- ❤ Wind rubber bands around the hard-boiled eggs in various directions. Be sure and leave spaces between the rubber bands.

- ❤ Put the egg dye in a bowl and mix it with water following the dye directions.

- ❤ Keep the eggs in the dye until they have reached your favorite color shade.

- ❤ Lift the eggs from the dye and place them on newspaper to dry. When dry, remove the rubber bands.

Try using natural dyes: coffee, cranberry juice, beets, onion skins, blueberry juice, and red cabbage.

❤   ❤   ❤

3. Deviled eggs are oftentimes an Easter special. Try this idea to create a different twist to the ol' egg: Instead of putting your boiled egg on its side to cut in half lengthwise, sit it up straight, cut a slice off the wide end so it sits up tall. Cut a slice off the narrow end and save, hollow out the egg and prepare according to your regular recipe. Restuff the egg and set the saved portion of the cooked white to use as a little hat atop the stuffed egg.

4. As Easter is an opportunity for new beginnings, approach this season with prayer, soul searching, and freshness (Psalm 139:23,24). I use this time to redo my flowerpots, put out the new ferns, and refresh and renew our home from winter into spring. It is a time to enjoy God's grace and goodness in sending His Son to address our iniquities.

5. In Ann Hibbard's book *Family Celebrations at Easter* she suggests: "Shoot the gospel straight with your children, speak on their terms, seek God together as a family....A heart that is open to God will soon be filled with a joy that spills over into the lives around it."

♥ 5 Family Traditions That Last a Lifetime

1. Take long walks down memory lane. View photo albums with your children. Tell them about your wedding day, tell them about the day they were born, show them the pictures as you help them learn about their history.

2. Create a mission statement for your family. When the children are older, sit down together and decide what you stand for, how you exemplify your beliefs, and how each family member matters.

3. Try Chip and Patti MacGregor's fun and tasty tip, from their book *Family Times*. One night, about ten minutes after bedtime, race into your children's rooms, flip on the light, and yell, "Pajama ride!" Wrap a blanket around them, place them in the car, and go to Dairy Queen for a hot fudge sundae. You will build an exciting and tasty memory.

4. Understand and follow your children's interests. My parents did a great job with this. My brother was a huge Dallas Cowboy fan, so we religiously watched their football games as well as visiting the Football Hall of Fame and several Super Bowls. On another note, I was a huge Donny Osmond fan. I lost count of the many concerts my parents sat through. We went to Utah in hopes of a face-to-face meeting. You see, it was the time and interest they took that allowed us to follow our dreams. (I did finally meet Donny, a real dream come true.)

5. Reading the Christmas story prior to opening gifts was a big part of our Christmas-sharing extravaganza. It focused our attention on what Christmas really means prior to us sharing our love gifts with each other. A casual supper (food again), the Christmas story, and prayer always preceded our exchange.

Mama's order was heavenly. It had to do with thoroughness...and taking plenty of time.

Susannah Lessard

💜 14 Steps to an Organized Household

1. Keep a tablet convenient and make notes.

2. If you do not want to forget, start writing things down. Sometimes not even this helps me. Read what you have written and follow through.

3. Keep the whole crew involved. When it is a group project, it is less apt to fall through the cracks.

4. Find a place to put your stuff. Assign family members baskets, shelves, drawers, whatever! This is so they can find their mail, their phone lists, their party invitations.

5. Be prepared.

6. Have a launching pad or a spot for placing the items you might need the next day. Keep wet-wipes, snacks, and an extra pair of earrings in your car, just in case.

7. Make a plan for attacking the disorganization. How do you eat an elephant? One bite at a time.

8. Spend smartly.

9. Make sure your money matters are in order and find a filing system that works for you.

10. When overwhelmed with all that must be accomplished, pick one item and start.

11. Simplify. Give items you do not need to someone who does. Keep a spot in your home for donations.

12. Take a break. If you see you are heading for overload, stop. Go to Starbucks or the mall. An overly-organized addict is not good for anyone.

13. My good friend and former college roommate, Kimber Andrews, mother of two girls, selected colorful ribbons and monogrammed the days of the week on them. She uses the ribbons to tie each day's outfit together, including socks and accessories.

14. Talk to God about it. He is a God of order. He will help you.

❤ 6 Strategies for Having More Family Time

1. Watch the clock. This will help you know where your time is going or has gone.

2. Do what you enjoy. Strong Families Study has done research over the past 20 years of 14,000 families. This study found that people regularly overcommitted themselves to things they did not enjoy doing.

3. Do not overbook your weekends. Much of our free time is lost making the weekends a mad dash of to-do's. Try keeping an ongoing to-do list so things can be accomplished a little at a time.

4. If you need help, do what you can to find it. If finances do not allow for this, try time exchanges with other moms or hiring an older high school student or hiring a retired neighbor when crunch times occur.

5. Try not to plan every minute. Spontaneous fun can sometimes make for the best times.

6. Turn off the television. Lie on the floor and read together, play games, or do a puzzle. This type of focused energy makes for great conversation.

💜 4 Ideas for Thanksgiving Treats

Remembering to be thankful every day is great, but there is one day each year when we pay extra attention to thankfulness. Thanksgiving is the praise holiday, the one day we stop and offer thanks to God for the many blessings He has given us throughout the year. The traditional table centerpiece, the cornucopia flowing with fruits and vegetables, is a symbol of the bountiful blessings we receive.

The Thanksgiving season is a perfect time to show people that you appreciate them. Make some of these treats as a special "thank you." Wrap each one in colored plastic wrap or tissue paper and tie it with a fall-colored ribbon. For each person include a note that says "I'm thankful for you because..." and fill in the blank.

Recipes

Gobble Gobble Cakes

Things You'll Need:

measuring cups
measuring spoons
sifter
2 large bowls
electric mixer
plastic wrap
rolling pin
turkey-shaped cookie cutter
cookie sheet
spatula

Ingredients:

5¼ cups all-purpose flour, sifted
½ teaspoon baking soda
1 cup (2 sticks) butter, softened
3 cups sugar
3 eggs
1 cup heavy cream
food coloring, optional

Directions:

1. In a large bowl, sift together flour and baking soda and set aside. If you don't want to mess up another bowl, sift the flour and baking soda onto waxed paper.

2. In a large bowl, cream the butter, gradually add the sugar and beat on low speed for two minutes.

3. Add the eggs one at a time, beating after each addition until thoroughly mixed.

4. If coloring the dough, add the food coloring to the cream before stirring it into the flour.

5. Add the flour mixture alternately with the cream. Beat only until smooth after each addition.

6. Divide the dough into quarters and wrap tightly in plastic wrap and refrigerate overnight.

7. Preheat the oven to 350°.

8. Using a floured rolling pin, roll out each part of the dough to a thickness of about ¼ inch on a floured surface, place your child's hand on the dough and cut around the shape using a plastic knife.

9. Place the hand shapes onto a cookie sheet, pull the thumb down to represent the turkey's head. (The four fingers will be the turkey's feathers.) Bake for 12 to 15 minutes, or until lightly browned.

10. Ice with your favorite fall-colored icings.

❤ ❤ ❤

Recipes

First Thanksgiving Popcorn Balls

Things You'll Need:

measuring cup
measuring spoons
double boiler
spoon
large bowl
waxed paper

Ingredients:

½ stick butter (4 tablespoons)
25 large marshmallows
1 teaspoon maple extract
8 cups popped popcorn
½ cup chocolate candy corns

Directions:

1. Place water in the bottom of the double boiler and place the second saucepan on the top.

2. Melt butter and marshmallows in the top saucepan over medium heat. Stir in the maple extract.

3. Place the popcorn in a large bowl that has been sprayed with cooking spray. Pour marshmallow-and-butter mixture onto the popcorn and stir thoroughly to combine. Fold in the candy corns.

4. Form into balls about three inches in diameter and place on wax paper to harden.

❤ ❤ ❤

Recipes

Tom Turkey Treats

Things You'll Need:

waxed paper
little paper plates
small plastic icing tip (found in cake section of grocery)

Ingredients:

8 vanilla wafers
4 large chocolate-covered candies (like Godiva or Russell Stover)
4 candy corns
4 Red Hots
white tube icing

Directions:

1. Using the white icing, glue the chocolate candy to the curved side of the vanilla wafer. (This forms the body of the turkey)

2. Using the white icing, glue the second vanilla wafer flat side to the back of the chocolate candy. (This forms the feathers at the back of the turkey.)

3. Starting at the top of the chocolate candy, glue the candy corn point down to start the face of the turkey.

4. Glue the red hot underneath the candy corn.

5. Place two dots of the white icing in the proper spot to be the turkey's eyes.

❤   ❤   ❤

Recipes

Harvest Hash

Things You'll Need:
small bags
raffia
large mixing bowl
wooden spoon

Ingredients:
1 box Bugle's Chips (to resemble cornucopia)
1 small bag pumpkin candies
2 cups caramel popcorn
1 cup golden raisins
2 cups small pretzels
1 cup peanuts

Directions:

1. Place all the ingredients into a large bowl and stir thoroughly.

2. Divide evenly into the fall-colored bags (glue several fall-colored silk leaves to the outside of your bag).

3. Tie the bag with the raffia and attach a "I'm thankful for you" note to the bag.

❤   ❤   ❤

December gifts—custom, ceremony, celebration, consecration—come to us wrapped up, not in tissue and ribbons, but in cherished memories.

Sarah Ban Breathnach

❤ 25 Homemade and Heartfelt Christmas Traditions

1. Plan a big Christmas shopping day the day after Thanksgiving.

2. Start burning pine-scented candles on December 1.

3. Go on a sleigh ride (even if your sleigh has to have wheels).

4. Do a yearly family wreath with each family member adding something that they are thankful for.

5. Begin eating every meal on Christmas china starting on December 1.

6. Organize a neighborhood cookie exchange.

7. Plan a progressive dessert party.

8. Turn out all the lights in the house and read Christmas stories by the tree.

9. Buy small gifts for a family in need, wrap them creatively, and leave them on their doorstep.

10. Wrap 25 little surprises for a nursing home patient. Deliver a big box filled with the inexpensive gifts, and ask them to open one each day for the remaining days in December.

11. Boil cinnamon sticks in apple juice for a holiday house aroma.

12. Create matching holiday T-shirts for each member of the family.

13. Buy every family member new red pajamas.

14. Make a two-story gingerbread house.

15. Go caroling, Dickens style.

16. Put a set of jingle bells on each entry door handle of your home.

17. Purchase a holiday doormat.

18. Sew Christmas charms to the tops of your stocking.

19. Hang mistletoe in the hallway and entryway of your home.

20. Enclose Christmas confetti in your Christmas cards.

21. Select a decorating theme for the season.

22. Address your Christmas cards the weekend after Thanksgiving.

23. Watch *White Christmas* as you wrap your Christmas gifts.

24. Keep a basket of gingerbread men wrapped in Christmas paper and ribbons by your door and offer one to guests as they leave your home.

25. Put on your favorite Christmas CDs and listen as you make homemade Christmas potpourri. Fill little cellophane bags and tie them onto Christmas packages.

❤   ❤   ❤

3 Ways to Be a Good Mom and a Good Friend Too

In *If You Ever Needed Friends, It's Now,* Leslie Parrott says, "It is one thing to start a friendship, it is quite another to maintain it, to stay on what C.S. Lewis called 'the same secret path'—especially as a parent. Even strong friendships require watering or they shrivel up and blow away." Here are three of the most important qualities every mom needs to consider for maintaining her friendships:

1. **Loyalty:** Loyal friends not only lend a hand when you're in need, they applaud your successes and cheer you on without envy when you prosper. Especially when that prosperity comes in the form of a tiny little life called a baby.

2. **Forgiveness:** Unless you are a saint, you are bound to offend every friend deeply at least once in the course of time—intentionally or unintentionally—and if the relationship survives, it will be because your friend forgives. The friends we keep the longest are the friends who forgive us the most. And the essence of true friendship is knowing what to overlook.

3. Honesty: True friends aren't afraid to be honest and they aren't afraid to be themselves. True friends follow Emerson's advice: "Better be a nettle in the side of your friend than his echo." Translation: If you are afraid of making enemies you'll never have true friends.

Mom Matters

- 💜 5 Ways to Make God First in Your Life

- 💜 4 Ways to Grow in God's Grace

- 💜 3 Ways to Find Joy

- 💜 5 Words of Encouragement to Help You Seize the Day

- 💜 4 Ways to Realness

- 💜 7 Simple Principles to Building Your Home with Encouragement and Love

- 💜 4 Ways to Establish Personal Peace

- 💜 7 Steps to Greater Health

- 💜 4 Ways to Transition to a "Stay-at-Home" Mom

- 💜 5 Things to Consider When You Have a "Working from Home" Office

- 💜 8 Ways to Streamline and Style-up Your Wardrobe

- 💜 8 "Little Luxuries" to Celebrate You

- 💜 7 Ways to Take a Daily Mini Vacation

- 💜 7 Ways to Achieve the Spirit of Femininity

- 💜 8 Ways to Stay in Shape

- 💜 8 Makeup Secrets to Keep You Cute

- 💜 20 Ways to Build Speaking Confidence

- 💜 25 Things Moms Need Most

Mom Matters

But seek first His kingdom and His righteousness;
and all these things shall be added to you.
Matthew 6:33

omen play multiple roles in life. Is it possible to perform them all well? Can we just simply have too much on our plates? Some people's existence reminds me of that paper plate commercial. A flimsy paper plate is piled full of entrees. In an attempt to satisfy, more and more is piled on the plate. But before reaching the table, the plate collapses under the numerous selections. The strong paper plate provides a solid foundation for the food and does not collapse. God provides a strong foundation for us. He encourages us to pile less on, but supports us and provides the strength for our overbooked lives.

In order for our families to be successful we, as wives and mothers, must be successful in knowing what is important for us as individuals and for our families. It ultimately boils down to priorities. Are your priorities in order? Setting priorities is a critical way to combat stress. The priorities you set can act as a compass for planning everything you do. Many of us do loads of good things, but are they the very best for you and your family? If the most important to-dos are accomplished first, it is easier to relax when everything is not completed in a day.

Once your priorities are concrete in your thought process, what's next? Focus. I find focusing to be one of the most difficult practices as a mother. My theory is that brain cells are reduced during delivery of a baby. Focus is one of my most challenging aspects of daily living. How does one deal with this? A carefully planned day spins into orbit at the onset of an ear infection or accident, so a mom must be willing to alter her schedule frequently.

Priorities for a woman pierce straight to the heart, especially when they are out of sync. Adjusting and attaining priorities is a daily decision—a decision that should involve daily placing your focus on God instead of on the circumstances at hand. Riding the merry-go-round of life often causes priorities to spin out of control. Striving to meet that next deadline, pushing to help that loved one, or volunteering for another project is a formula for priority paralysis.

When I begin to feel like the little ball that is consistently batted around in a pinball machine, hitting off of this corner and slamming into that corner, I know God is not in control. As the bells and whistles begin to ring, I realize I am following my will and probably not God's.

This is a critical time for self-evaluation. A restructuring of what is truly important and a renewed focus toward eternity must become my new focus.

Priorities are necessary tools for our lives. They are the first stimulus to action. What are your life choices? "Blessed are the meek" Jesus said (Matthew 5:5 NIV). The word "meek" means patient and is meant to describe a strong person following God's direction. God gives us power under control and strength with direction.

When I suffer from priority paralysis, I stop, quickly write down my priorities, and rearrange the thought process fogging the issue. A powerful prayer, a focus on obedience, and a heart choice slow the merry-go-round and calm the spirit. I see these as simple steps which enable me to be what I was created to be.

A better me makes a better we, a better we makes a better parenting team, and a better parenting team produces a better family. As a small stone is thrown into a pond, the ripples roll throughout the water's surface. So what you might consider a small influence, or a small stone thrown into the waters of life, has the capacity to impact many.

Before you begin to look at your personal priorities, take time to pray for direction and clarity. In Charles Hummel's book *The Tyranny of the Urgent,* he tells us that we desire to do important things, but often get sidetracked by urgent things. (Our daily to-dos: food, cleaning, carpool, laundry, and making it on time to ballet.) Mr. Hummel urges us to wait for direction from the Lord to keep our priorities in place.

Self-evaluation is a valuable way to accomplish a priority check. You will need a pad, scheduled time alone, and your Bible. What is most important to you? How do you spend your time? Taking time to reflect on these things will help solidify what matters most.

There is only so much sand in the hourglass. Who gets it? This simple yet thought-provoking exercise can be an eye-opener. Try this prayerfully and see how God speaks to you.

On a sheet of paper make four columns using each of the following questions as a section heading:

1. What do you want to do?

2. What do you want to be?

3. What do you want to have?

4. Who do you want to help?

Write your answers beneath each heading. Then, narrow your answers to a three-word phrase that sums up your columns. When you have three words, select one word that represents you. While obviously our existence is not this simple, this is a good way to view the mirror of your heart.

You might be thinking, *Is there time for me? Does it matter what I think, want, plan?* You better believe it matters. Mom matters. It is vital that you take care of yourself. Moms are familiar with sponges, so look at it this way. If a sponge is too full, will it be able to perform its job satisfactorily? You are not as effective in any aspect of your life when you have soaked up more than your share. Exhaustion, stress, hurriedness, and overbooked schedules take their toll. Occasionally you need to do your family a favor, and give yourself some time. Time for a manicure, bubble bath, trip to the bookstore, or whatever makes you feel you have had a break. If your priorities are firm, your direction is clear, and your restful times are less stressful because you know where you are going.

After you have reviewed your thoughts and feelings, established your priorities and taken some personal time, you are prepared to move to the next level. When evaluating your strongest thoughts and deepest feelings, it might take days or weeks to make decisions. When the answers are not obvious, try these suggestions from Paul Little's booklet *Affirming the Will of God:*

1. Pray with an attitude of obedience to God.

2. Look for guidance from Scripture.

3. Obtain information from competent sources.

4. Obtain advice from people knowledgeable about the issue.

5. Make the decision without second-guessing God.

Taking the time and energy to chart your course in life is not an exercise in futility; it is an exercise in focusing on what is truly important. The key here is determination to find a place for your personal life, time for God to fill your tank, time for God to give you direction, and time for growth to keep you sharp.

Here are several ways to take care of you while establishing and holding on to what is truly important.

As the deer pants for the water brooks,
so my soul pants for Thee, O God.
Psalm 42:1

♥ 5 Ways to Make God First in Your Life

1. Decide that you want to make Him first.

2. Prayer.

3. Bible study. Knowing God and His attributes allows you to make and keep God first.

4. Surround yourself with friends that share the desire to make God first in their life. When you share common desires, you can encourage each other along the way.

5. Find an accountability partner and share your heart, your prayers, and your trust.

♥ 4 Ways to Grow in God's Grace

How do you establish a root system anchored deep in God's Word? In *A Woman After God's Own Heart*™, Elizabeth George offers us insight into aspects of a root system produced by regular, faithful Bible study:

1. Roots are unseen. You'll want to set aside time in solitude—"underground"—to immerse yourself in God's Word and grow in Him.

2. Roots are for taking in. Alone and with your Bible in hand, you'll want to take in and feed upon the truths of the Word of God and ensure your spiritual growth.

3. Roots are for storage. As you form the habit of looking into God's Word, you'll find a vast reservoir of divine hope and strength forming for the rough times.

4. Roots are for support. Do you want to stand strong in the Lord? To stand firm against the pressures of life? The routine care of your roots through exposure to God's Word will cultivate you into a remarkable woman of endurance.

3 Ways to Find Joy

In Lindsey O'Connor's book *If Mama Ain't Happy, Ain't Nobody Happy,* she offers you practical tips for living with joy. "Joy itself is never something we can practice, but we can practice living a lifestyle that includes disciplines conducive to joyfulness." Here are a few of her suggestions:

1. Disciplines of Lifestyle—Establish a life of simplicity. Do what you can to reduce barren business.

2. Disciplines of the Whole Person—Once steps are taken towards a simpler life, we can live a life of joy when focusing on what we feed our mind; how we exercise; and how we rest our mind, body, and spirit.

3. Disciplines of Labor—People who greatly enjoy life tend to be those who are involved in the disciplines of service and meaningful work balanced with fun.

♥ 5 Words of Encouragement to Help You Seize the Day

Seize: To take possession of. Confiscate. Apprehend. Capture. Grasp.

Let this simple acrostic help remind you to seize each day and delight in its potential.

1. S—Supernatural

Walk in the supernatural. What is your spiritual temperature? Are you getting your strength from above or are you running on empty? These simple steps can fill you up again.

- ♥ Receive Jesus Christ as your Savior, as your gift from God.

- ♥ Do not doubt your salvation. It is by God's grace that you have this gift.

- ♥ Allow God to control each area of your life and heart.

- ♥ Confess your sins, quickly, and get on with it.

- ♥ Focus on His direction for your life. "In all your ways acknowledge Him, and He shall direct your paths" Proverbs 3:6 NKJV.

- ♥ Find and live by your life's verse. This is mine:

Yet those who wait for the LORD will gain new strength; they will mount up with wings like eagles, they will run and not get tired, they will walk and not become weary.

Isaiah 40:31

2. E—Enthusiasm

Are you enthusiastic in your life ministry? Enthusiasm is joy bubbling over. It is hard to be enthusiastic in the mundane, so our focus must be our eternal perspective so that our enthusiasm stays strong.

Years may wrinkle the skin, but a lack of enthusiasm will wrinkle the soul.

3. I—Intimacy

Do you have intimate relationships? Ones where you can bare your soul, feed your soul, and nourish your existence? First, intimate relationship should be with God. How are you getting nourished for seizing the day?

4. Z—Zeal

Are you zealous in your approach to your day? Do you have a zeal for God? He (or she) who has no fire or zeal in himself (herself) cannot warm others.

5. E—Endurance

Endurance is a key factor in the life of women. Have you noticed? How can you capture endurance when you are already tired?

1. Keep looking to the finish line.

2. Keep approaching your days with an eternal perspective.

Therefore, since we have so great a cloud of witnesses surrounding us, let us also lay aside every encumbrance, and the sin which so easily entangles us, and let us run with endurance the race that is set before us.

Hebrews 12:1

There is no hope for any of us until we confess our helplessness. Then we are in a position to receive grace... so long as we see ourselves as competent, we do not qualify.

Elisabeth Elliot

💜 4 Ways to Realness

Brenda Waggoner, licensed counselor and author of *The Velveteen Woman,* makes these suggestions for what it means to be real:

1. Cultivate inner beauty. Physical beauty is not lasting, nor is it a reflection of your goodness or worth.

2. Comparisons are not helpful. We always lose when we compare ourselves with other women. Each of us is a unique creation, precious to God. Nothing can compare to that.

3. Surrender to God. Do not be controlled by dominant people around you, Nana's who like to tidy us up! Do not think you are the one in control.

4. Accept God's love as an unconditional, lavish gift. We cannot perform well enough to earn it, learn enough about it to fully comprehend it, or deserve it. All we can really do is accept it. Welcome God's love each morning by saying out loud, "God, I accept Your love for me!"

❤ 7 Simple Principles to Building Your Home with Encouragement and Love

Karol Ladd, mother of two, author, speaker, and friend explains in her book *The Power of a Positive Mom* seven ways to offer encouragement, love, and positive parenting:

1. The power of encouragement—Be an encourager through your words, expectations, and smile.

2. The power of prayer—Cast your cares on the Lord and establish an effective prayer time for your family.

3. The power of a good attitude—Stop whining and practice an attitude of gratitude each day. Learn to grow through the challenges of life.

4. The power of strong relationships—Continually work to build better relationships with your husband, your children, your friends, and mentors in your life.

5. The power of your example—Remember that your life is a living book of lessons which your children are reading every day. Live out the qualities you want to see in them.

6. The power of strong moral standards—Anchor your children in God's principles for life, which are found in the Bible.

7. The power of love and forgiveness—Show God's love and compassion through your training and discipline.

You will keep him in perfect peace
whose mind is stayed on You.

Isaiah 26:3 NKJV

💜 4 Ways to Establish Personal Peace

1. In Donna Otto's book *The Stay-at-Home Mom*, she says, "Ordering your personal life is primarily a spiritual matter." Begin your day with prayer. Prayer for guidance as a wife, mother, daughter, friend, and neighbor.

2. Practice peaceful things. Light candles, take a long bath, take a quiet walk, schedule yourself some time so you can be a better you.

3. Memorize Scripture verses about peace.

4. Ask God for His peace.

Priority Verses

Delight yourself in the LORD; and He will give you the desires of your heart.
Psalm 37:4

But seek first his kingdom and his righteousness, and all of these things will be given to you as well.
Matthew 6:33 NIV

For physical training is of some value, but godliness has value for all things, holding promise for both the present life and the life to come.
1 Timothy 4:8 NIV

Trust in the LORD with all your heart and lean not on your own understanding; in all your ways acknowledge him, and he will make your paths straight.
Proverbs 3:5,6 NIV

Be still, and know that I am God; I will be exalted among the nations; I will be exalted in the earth.
Psalm 46:10 NIV

I have hidden your word in my heart that I might not sin against you.
Psalm 119:11 NIV

Let the word of Christ dwell in you richly as you teach and admonish one another with all wisdom, and as you sing psalms, hymns and spiritual songs with gratitude in your hearts to God. And whatever you do, whether in word or deed, do it all in the name of the Lord Jesus, giving thanks to God the Father through him.
Colossians 3:16,17 NIV

So then, banish anxiety from your heart and cast off the troubles of your body, for youth and vigor are meaningless.
Ecclesiastes 11:10 NIV

♥ 7 Steps to Greater Health

In Stormie O'Martian's book *Greater Health God's Way*, she offers seven steps to inner and outer beauty. She explains, "Those who view their body as a dwelling place for the Holy Spirit of God, and, accordingly, treat it with respect and care, are best able to adapt to God's ways." Try Stormie's seven steps:

1. Peaceful living.

2. Pure food.

3. Proper exercise.

4. Plenty of water.

5. Prayer and fasting.

6. Periods of fresh air and sunshine.

7. Perfect rest.

♥ 4 Ways to Transition to a "Stay-at-Home" Mom

Cheryl Gochnauer, author of *So You Want to Be a Stay-at-Home Mom* and weekly author of the *Homebodies* column at www.homebodies.com, explains "When constructing your stay-at-home dream house, include these vital planks:

1. A detailed plan.

2. Why are you coming home?

3. What do you hope to accomplish?

4. How will you make the transition financially, emotionally, and career-wise?"

Says Gochnauer, "Know these answers, and your house will stand strong when brisk winds blow."

❤ 5 Things to Consider When You Have a "Working from Home" Office

When your office space is limited, organization and efficiency are a must. Try these "easy on the budget" suggestions to create workable office space:

1. Two metal file cabinets and an old door (minus the hardware) can double as a desk in a pinch. Use a staple gun to affix a pretty sheet around the edge of the door and the metal cabinets will not show.

2. Shop estate sales for a computer armoire. Insert your computer, printer, a ream of paper, and a business card holder and you are set. This provides one piece to accommodate everything, and it closes to camouflage your work when not being used.

3. If your files are too numerous, or you need a clutter buster, purchase some metal shelving for your garage. The garage or a rented storage unit are excellent places for files you do not need to access frequently.

4. Big baskets work great for your in box, to-do files, and out box. They can also be picked up and stored quickly should entertaining or reducing clutter be necessary.

5. A good filing system is the heart of efficient office management.

Let not your adornment be merely external...let it be the hidden person of the heart, with the imperishable quality of a gentle and quiet spirit, which is precious in the sight of God.

1 Peter 3:3-4

♥ 8 Ways to Streamline and Style-Up Your Wardrobe

When you dress each morning, what do you reach for again and again? Your uniform or comfort clothes? Busy lives created the need for clothes to go from weekday to weekend, to be travel-friendly yet classy. A true operation for a high level of mix-and-match coordination. Brenda Gardner, a stylish mother of an infant and four-year-old, offers these thoughts: "I try to shop sales at my favorite stores, buying better quality at a discount, hopefully! Tailored clothes seem to work best, preferably in monochromatic colors. These become wardrobe stretchers. I am not afraid to wear my favorite clothes over and over. As long as I feel good in the outfit, why save it? Wear it!"

1. Perform a closet inventory. Divide a simple notebook into sections like blouses, pants, and so on. List what you have and give away what you never wear. Take this

notebook when you shop to help you remember what you do and do not need.

2. Purchase a string of pearls. They don't have to be real, just elegant. Pearls are stylish with jeans as well as that perfect black dress.

3. Purchase several sweater sets in solid colors to wear with alternating skirts and pants.

4. Invest extra money in wardrobe staples such as black pants, a black skirt, crisp white blouses, and a navy blazer.

5. Update your accessories. Keep the design simple yet classic.

6. Consider these things when you are reviewing your wardrobe: your lifestyle, your personal style, your body style, your color style, and your comfort.

7. Make sure to always have a crisp white shirt.

8. Here are a few more tips from another very stylish friend, Leah Eiden. She coordinates national conventions, writes, edits, and runs an organized home.

> You do not have to spend a great deal of money to look stylish. By being educated and organized you can achieve style on a budget. First, research styles, colors, and fabrics by reading magazines, looking at mail-order catalogs, window shopping, and even

watching anchors on television news programs. Second, based on your preferences, choose items that realistically reflect your lifestyle. Third, jot a list of items you have decided to purchase, including their regular department store prices. By knowing quality and prices you can shop discount stores and outlets early in the season and not wait for end-of-season sales at department stores. Fourth, shop! Purchase items which fit well, are flattering, suit your lifestyle, meet your budget, and are on your list. If you are indecisive about an item, the answer is probably no. Save that money for something you really want later. Complete every outfit with a smile. Not only will you look better, but you will feel better too!

♥ 8 "Little Luxuries" to Celebrate You

1. Schedule an afternoon at a bookstore, one with a coffee shop inside. Sip and read while you relax.

2. Attend a weekend retreat. Many churches offer retreats for women only. Also, MOPS (Mothers of Preschoolers, website: www.mops.org) and Hearts-at-Home (website: www.hearts-at-home.org) offer national and regional conferences.

3. Join a Bible study that digs deep into the biblical aspects of the issues you face.

4. Begin a bi-monthly book club in your home. Read books that help you grow as a person and as a mom. The friendships you develop with other members are an added bonus.

5. Schedule a massage following a particularly hectic week. It can be your light at the end of the tunnel.

6. Teatime is relaxing. Can you gulp hot tea? No! Isn't that great!! Sit down, relax, reflect, restore. Here is a little poem from Sarah's preschool teacher, Mrs. Cormany, to help you stop and cope during a hectic day.

> *I give you this gift today.*
> *I'll try to be good in every way.*
> *But should you get*
> *Impatient with me,*
> *Sit down, relax and*
> *Have a cup of tea.*

7. Take a daily vacation. Everyone needs down time, time to do nothing, even if it is only 15 to 20 minutes. We all need time when we aren't racing, running, and ranting. This is when the body slows down and the mind is free to relax and be creative. Remember, you cannot multitask relaxation.

8. Find peace. It starts with establishing priorities, releasing too many activities, conquering clutter, and being grateful. Thoreau said, "I love a broad margin to my life." In other words, the less packed into a day, the better. For the sake of sanity, switching gears is the best

option. Postpone the errands, cancel a play date, order a take-out dinner, skip an evening to-do. These are small luxuries that make a big difference.

Come to Me, all who are weary and heavy-laden,
and I will give you rest.
Matthew 11:28

7 Ways to Take a Daily Mini Vacation

1. Smile.

2. Relax in a rocking chair.

3. Breathe deeply.

4. Alternate activities.

5. Fill the bathroom with lots of candles and take a long, hot bubble bath.

6. Snuggle in a bathrobe while reading a great book.

7. Listen to your favorite classical music while sipping a warm cup of coffee.

7 Ways to Achieve the Spirit of Femininity

In Emilie Barnes' book *The Spirit of Loveliness*, she explains how to enjoy your femininity: "The most feminine woman is one with an eye and ear for others and a heart for God. We honor God when we rejoice in our femininity and let it transform the world around us. Femininity is so much more than lace and flowers. A woman with the spirit of femininity is a woman with a teachable heart."

1. Next time you take a walk, pick a few flowers. Tuck them in a vase by your bed…on your husband's side.

2. If you work from home, consider your everyday "look." Is it casual or just sloppy? (Ouch! I am sitting in front of my computer in my mismatched workout clothes.) Why not wake up ten minutes early to fix yourself for the people you love most?

3. Gain inspiration by reading stories about great women, such as Ruth Bell Graham, Elisabeth Elliot, and Barbara Bush.

4. Hang a wind chime out on the patio and enjoy its music on breezy evenings.

5. Enjoy a bubble bath by candlelight with soft classical music in the background.

6. Go to Victoria's Secret and purchase some pretty lingerie.

7. Schedule "happys for your heart." I personally love facials and manicures.

It isn't the big pleasures that count most;
it's making a great deal out of the little ones.

Jean Webster

🖤 8 Ways to Stay in Shape

1. Walk together as a family.

2. Drink eight glasses of water per day.

3. When you have "put on a few," try eating a fiber-enriched cereal with fruit for dinner for one week to help diminish those extra pounds. Stay away from heavy sweets that week too.

4. Do leg lifts while you watch television.

5. Find a weight accountability partner and set a walking date with that person twice a week.

6. Select several flavorful lower-fat recipes. Try *Cooking Light* magazine for some good ideas.

7. Use stairs instead of elevators or escalators whenever available.

8. If you love rich desserts, try just eating half. This will address the sweet tooth and you won't feel deprived.

Wash and perfume yourself, and put on your best clothes.
Ruth 3:3 NIV

💗 8 Makeup Secrets to Keep You Cute

1. Wash and moisturize your face twice a day. Be sure and start your makeup application with a clean canvas.

2. Instead of typical toners, where you pay a lot for packaging, use witch hazel, a time-tested over-the-counter astringent.

3. Try Vaseline to smooth unruly eyebrows and on your lips for a healthy shine. This also works great to soften cuticles and as a nail buffer.

4. Get a professional facial once in a while. If that does not fit into the family budget, wash your face and use an astringent. Boil some water on the stove and then turn off the burner and place your face over the water to steam. This will open pores. Then try your favorite deep-cleansing mask. Once the mask has done its thing, use the astringent again, then moisturize.

5. Clean your makeup brushes and powder puffs often.

6. Purchase an inexpensive pencil sharpener for your eyeliners and lipliners. A sharp tip makes all the difference in your makeup application.

7. The key to successful daytime makeup is restraint. Concentrate on blending skin tone, adding only a touch of color to the face and definition to the eyes and mouth for an effective "no-makeup" look.

8. To keep your hands soft and pretty, do not overwash. Wear latex gloves if your hands are going to be in water for long periods of time, then moisturize, moisturize, moisturize. When I used to travel, I would cover clean hands with Bag Balm (available at feed stores and, yes, used on cows udders), and sleep in white gloves. This was a great conditioning for softer-looking hands.

❤ 20 Ways to Build Speaking Confidence

As women and as mothers, we are often called upon to speak, lead, coordinate, and anticipate large groups and gatherings. Here are some tips from Ken Bradford's The Leaders Course for speaking confidently in public.

1. Let yourself *be yourself.*

2. Give yourself permission to *try out* different selves, but do not command yourself to make a major change. Set realistic expectations. Break big goals into bite-sized pieces.

3. Allow yourself to *have* and *express* feelings. You have to feel the lows to enjoy the highs.

4. Allow yourself to take some *personal space.* And take some personal time. Make dates with yourself. Enjoy your own company.

5. Allow yourself to move, grow, and *change.*

6. *Give support to others* and learn to *accept* it in return.

7. *Allow* yourself to make *mistakes*.

8. *Express* valid personal wants and needs.

9. *Take responsibility* for your thoughts, feelings, and ideas by using *I messages*. They keep communication lines open.

10. *Accepting your body* the way it is, is the first step to changing it.

11. Learn to say *no* without feeling guilty.

12. Take time each day *to relax*. Rest before you become tired.

13. Become *aware* of what things are *reinforcing* to you. Use them. Most of us are tuned-in to reinforcements for other people (both colleagues and clients), but we do not think enough about what is rewarding to us.

14. Be aware of your energy *cycles*. Do not fight them, use them.

15. Allow yourself to *dream*.

16. *Catch yourself* doing things right and acknowledge it.

17. *Reframe problems* into *challenges*.

18. Figure out your *negative patterns* and re-organize your rewards in those modes.

19. *Exercise* your whole body every day.

20. *Pray* for what you really want.

25 Things Moms Need Most

1. A sanity check.

2. To know that I am normal.

3. To know that I am a good mother.

4. Acceptance.

5. Encouragement.

6. Support.

7. Time.

8. Time with my husband.

9. Time off.

10. Time alone.

11. Time with God.

12. Patience.

13. More energy.

14. A break.

15. A nap.

16. Adult conversation.

17. A best friend.

18. Someone to understand how I feel.

19. A housekeeper.

20. A secretary.

21. A nanny.

22. A dishwasher that loads itself and a vacuum that cleans by remote control.

23. A vacation.

24. Friends.

25. To know that being a mother is important.

From *What Every Mom Needs* by Elisa Morgan and Carol Kuykendal.

What Matters Most?

We have looked at our husbands, our children, our home, our family and friends, and ourselves. Ideas, lists, recipes, suggestions, quotes, and biblical truths *can* make a difference. However, none of this will make a difference if you as an individual, a woman, a wife, a mother, a daughter, a sister, a niece, or a friend do not first realize the eternal importance of a personal relationship with Jesus Christ.

When you make the decision, through the grace of God, to live a life that pleases God, you are better equipped to guide and provide the loving support your family needs. It is very simple. Jesus already did all the work by coming to this world and dying on a cross so that we may choose eternal life.

For God so loved the world, that He gave
His only begotten Son, that whoever believes in Him
should not perish, but have eternal life.
John 3:16

This is what matters most for you and your family. My prayer for you is that you will make the decision to let His love touch your life. I know you will make a difference.

Recommended Resources

Husbands Matter

Elise Arndt, *A Mother's Time* (Colorado Springs, CO: Cook Communications Ministries, 1987).

Gary Chapman, *The Five Love Languages* (Chicago, IL: Northfield Publishing, a division of Moody Press, 1992).

Becky Freeman, *Chocolate Chili Pepper Love* (Eugene, OR: Harvest House, 2000).

Edwina Patterson, *Redeeming the Time With My Husband* (Heart for the Home Ministry at www.heart-for-home.org).

Jill Savage, *Professionalizing Motherhood* (Hearts-at-Home at www.hearts-at-home.org).

Gary Smalley and John Trent, *The Language of Love* (Pomona, CA: Focus on the Family, 1988).

Children Matter

Emilie Barnes, *Emilie's Creative Home Organizer* (Eugene, OR: Harvest House, 1995).

Ludwig Bemelmans, *Madeline* (New York, NY: Penguin Putnam, 1958).

Eric Carle, *The Very Hungry Caterpillar* (New York, NY: Penguin Putnam, Inc., Philomel, 1969).

Saxton Freymann and Joost Elffers, *How Are You Peeling?* (New York, NY: Scholastic, Inc., Arthur A. Levine Books, 1999).

Gloria Gaither and Shirley Dobson, *Let's Make a Memory* (Nashville, TN: Word Publishing, 1983).

Jan Karon, *Miss Fannie's Hat* (Minneapolis, MN: Augsberg Fortress Publishers, 1999).

Gracie Malone, "Can We Talk?" in *Moody Magazine,* Nov/Dec 1997.

Maurice Sendak, *Where the Wild Things Are* (New York, NY: HarperCollins, 1964).

Home Matters

Emilie Barnes, *Welcome Home* (Eugene, OR: Harvest House, 1997).

Chris Madden, *Chris Madden's Guide to Personalizing Your Home* (New York, NY: Clarkson Potter, 1997).

Family & Friends Matter

Cheri Fuller, *When Families Pray* (Sisters, OR: Multnomah Publishers, 1999).

Ann Hibbard, *Family Celebrations at Easter* (Ada, MI: Baker Books, 1994).

Ellie Kay, *Shop, Save, and Share* (Minneapolis, MN: Bethany House, 1998).

Leslie Parrott, *If You Ever Needed Friends, It's Now* (Grand Rapids, MI: Zondervan Publishing, 2000).

Mimi Wilson and Mary Beth Lagerborg, *Table Talk* (Wheaton, IL: Tyndale House, 2001).

Mom Matters

Emilie Barnes, *The Spirit of Loveliness* (Eugene, OR: Harvest House, 1992).

Elizabeth George, *A Woman After God's Own Heart* (Eugene, OR: Harvest House, 1997).

Cheryl Gochnauer, *So You Want to Be a Stay-at-Home Mom* (Downers Grove, IL: InterVarsity Press, 1999).

Charles Hummel, *The Tyranny of the Urgent* (Downers Grove, IL: InterVarsity Press, 1984).

Karol Ladd, *The Power of a Positive Mom* (West Monroe, LA: Howard Publishing, 2001).

Paul Little, *Affirming the Will of God* (Downers Grove, IL: Intervarsity Press, 1971).

Elise Morgan and Carol Kuykendal, *What Every Mom Needs* (Grand Rapids, MI: Zondervan Publishing, 1995).

Lindsey O'Connor, *If Mama Ain't Happy, Ain't Nobody Happy* (Eugene, OR: Harvest House, 1996).

Stormie Omartian, *Greater Health God's Way* (Eugene, OR: Harvest House, 1999).

Donna Otto, *The Stay-at-Home Mom* (Eugene, OR: Harvest House, 1997).

Brenda Waggoner, *The Velveteen Woman* (Colorado Springs, CO: Cook Communications Ministries, 1999).

For information about booking
Jane Jarrell to speak, contact:

Speak Up Speaker Services
1614 Edison Shores Place
Port Huron, MI 48060-3374

phone: 810-982-0898

e-mail: speakupinc@aol.com

Visit Jane's website and
share your ideas:
www.janejarrell.com

Other Good Harvest House Reading

Holiday Hugs
by Jane Jarrell
Give a special mom the gift of holiday sanity and creativity with this collection of Christmas ideas, including kids' crafts, tree trimmings, simple gift ideas, and holiday recipes.

Love You Can Touch
by Jane Jarrell
As Christians, one of the greatest gifts we can give to others is to show Christ's love tangibly. This attractive, practical book is filled with great ideas for ministering to others through food, gifts, kind words, and good deeds.

Mom's Little Helper Series
by Jane Jarrell
31 Ideas for Spreading Love at Lunch
26 Ways to Say "I Love You"
50 Ways to a Thankful Heart

The Power of a Praying™ Parent
by Stormie Omartian
Popular author and singer Stormie Omartian offers 30 easy-to-read chapters that focus on specific areas of prayers for parents.

If Mama Ain't Happy, Ain't Nobody Happy
by Lindsey O'Connor
"Happiness is overrated—go for joy!" encourages author Lindsey O'Connor. Includes chapters on choosing contentment, creating an atmosphere of joy, modeling joy to children, and discovering the disciplines of joyful people.

Peanut Butter Kisses and Mudpie Hugs
by Becky Freeman
From choosing furniture that camouflages peanut butter and jelly to her son's comment, "I'm so glad you aren't sensible like other kids' moms," Becky delightfully presents family moments that highlight God's loving presence.

Chocolate Chili Pepper Love
by Becky Freeman
Finding humor and hope amid the clutter of kids and romantic moments gone wrong, Becky celebrates the journey of marriage.

A Child's Garden of Prayer
by Steve & Becky Miller
A Child's Garden of Prayer includes bedtime prayers, mealtime prayers, Christmas prayers, and "just because" prayers of thanksgiving. Read-along rhymes help turn little hearts toward God with each new day.